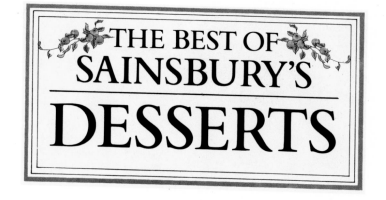

THE BEST OF SAINSBURY'S
DESSERTS

THE BEST OF
SAINSBURY'S
DESSERTS

CONTENTS

CONTRIBUTORS

Main author: Carole Handslip

Other contributing authors: Caroline Ellwood, Gwyneth Loveday, Wendy Godfrey, Rhona Newman, Julia Roles, Mary Reynolds and Norma MacMillan

Special photography: Paul Williams

NOTES

Standard spoon measurements are used in all recipes
1 tablespoon = one 15 ml spoon
1 teaspoon = one 5 ml spoon
All spoon measures are level.

Size 3 eggs should be used unless otherwise stated.

Ovens should be preheated to the specified temperature.

For all recipes, quantities are given in both metric and imperial measures. Follow either set but not a mixture of both, because they are not interchangeable.

Published exclusively for
J Sainsbury plc
Stamford House
Stamford Street
London SE1 9LL
by Reed Consumer Books Limited
Michelin House
81 Fulham Road
London SW3 6RB
and Auckland, Melbourne,
Singapore and Toronto

First published in Great Britain in 1985
Reprinted 1986, 1990, 1991, 1993

© Reed International Books Limited 1985

ISBN 0 86178 334 4

Produced by Mandarin Offset
Printed and bound in Hong Kong

INTRODUCTION

It is of course essential to plan your menu so that the dessert is appropriate for the meal and the circumstances. For example, try to balance a rich and satisfying main course with a light dessert, probably a fruity dessert, or perhaps a refreshing sorbet. With a lighter main course, a sumptuous gâteau or pastry-based dessert would complete the meal more satisfactorily. It goes without saying that on a cold winter's day a warming pie or a hot, crunchy crumble will be much appreciated. Ice creams, sorbets and frozen desserts are naturally perfect for those hot summer's days.

While I spend a lot of time writing about the more exotic puddings, I really prefer the clever application of simple ideas. In view of current opinions regarding diet, I think it is a good idea to avoid eating too much sugar and cream. I am especially fond of the lighter fruit-based desserts.

A colourful salad of fruits in season is one of the most popular desserts, but try serving it in a more imaginative manner than the usual glass bowl; use half a pineapple shell for a strawberry and pineapple salad, or a melon shell to hold scoops of melon, sliced kiwi fruit and seedless grapes, for example. To enhance the flavour, add a dash of liqueur.

Remember that the finishing touches make all the difference to the final result. Piped cream always gives a professional touch, but to be effective, really requires quite a lot of practice – try it out using mashed potato instead of cream until you have mastered the art. On the other hand, a delicate sprig of mint or lemon balm, attractive chocolate shapes or a little of the same fruit as that used in the recipe, could be sufficient to make your dessert a visual triumph.

Although I tend to prefer light fruity desserts, I have to admit that there are occasions when a really rich "gooey" pudding is just the thing, so I've included some of these too – Black Forest Gâteau, Chocolate Roulade, Profiteroles and Pavlova, to name but a few. These treats, well prepared, will guarantee a successful climax to your special meal.

I hope you enjoy the variety of recipes in this collection and I wish you success with your entertaining.

Carole Handslip.

FRUIT DESSERTS

Fresh fruity desserts are the perfect finish to a rich meal. Cool, refreshing and quick to prepare, they are especially good in summer when appetites wane and the desire to spend time in the kitchen vanishes!

Always use fresh fruits in season and, if you have a freezer, make the most of it. Store away some of those delectable short season fruits – such as cherries, raspberries and redcurrants – for winter treats.

Summer is the ideal time for fruit salads, as the choice of fresh fruit at this time of year is endless. The season's luxuries include cherries, peaches, strawberries and apricots. Autumn is the time to make the most of English tree fruits – apples, pears and plums. You will find plenty of exciting ideas for using these fruits in this chapter – refreshing alternatives to the ubiquitous apple pie!

Although winter is not the best time for home produced fruit, there are plenty of imported citrus fruits and exotic tropical fruits to choose from. Look out for lychees, guavas, passion fruit, kiwi fruit and the more familiar pineapples and bananas. These fruits complement each other perfectly in fruit salads. When fresh fruits are in short supply and expensive, opt for those tasty desserts which make use of dried fruits; apricots, figs, apples and dates, for example.

Most of the desserts in this chapter are delicious with cream, but for a lighter, healthier alternative try serving with refreshing yogurt or Crémets (see page 20), or simply serve plain to enjoy the full flavour of the fruit.

MELON, GRAPE AND KIWI FRUIT SALAD

1 large Galia melon
125 g (4 oz) green grapes, skinned and pipped
3 kiwi fruit, thinly sliced
1 × 312 g (11 oz) can lychees, drained
2 apples, peeled, cored and thinly sliced
3 tablespoons kirsch
mint sprigs to decorate

Cut a thin slice from the base of the melon so that it stands firmly. Cut the top off the melon, remove the seeds and discard. Scoop out the flesh into small balls, using a melon baller or teaspoon. Reserve the shell.

Place the melon balls and remaining fruits in a bowl, sprinkle with the kirsch, cover and chill.

Place the melon shell on a serving plate. Pile the fruit into the melon and decorate with mint sprigs.
Serves 4 to 6

SUMMER SALAD

1 pineapple
2 oranges, segmented
125 g (4 oz) strawberries, halved
125 g (4 oz) black grapes, halved and pipped
120 ml (4 fl oz) white wine
1 tablespoon clear honey
1 ripe pear
1 large banana
lemon balm leaves to decorate (optional)

Cut the pineapple in half lengthways, remove the flesh and cut into pieces, discarding the centre core; reserve the pineapple shells. Place the pineapple flesh in a bowl with the oranges, strawberries and grapes.

Mix the wine and honey together and pour over the fruit.

Core and slice the pear into the bowl; slice the banana and add to the bowl. Toss the fruit with the wine until well coated.

Turn into the pineapple shells and chill. Decorate with lemon balm if available, and serve with whipped cream.
Serves 6 to 8

PINEAPPLE AND LYCHEE SALAD

1 large pineapple
1 × 312 g (11 oz) can lychees, drained
125 g (4 oz) strawberries, halved
2 tablespoons icing sugar, sifted
4 tablespoons kirsch
lemon balm leaves to decorate (optional)

Cut the top off the pineapple and reserve. Carefully scoop out the flesh, using a serrated grapefruit knife and a spoon. Cut the flesh into chunks and place in a bowl. Add the lychees and strawberries. Sprinkle with the icing sugar and kirsch, mix well and leave to soak for 2 hours in the refrigerator.

Spoon the fruit and juice into the pineapple shell and decorate with lemon balm if possible.
Serves 6 to 8

MELON WITH RASPBERRIES

350 g (12 oz) raspberries
1 tablespoon icing sugar, sifted
3 tablespoons Grand Marnier
2 Charentais melons, chilled

Combine the raspberries in a bowl with the icing sugar and liqueur. Leave to soak for 2 hours.

Cut the melons in half, scoop out and discard the seeds. Cut a thin slice from the base of each half so that they stand firmly. Spoon the raspberries into the melon halves and serve immediately.
Serves 4

Raspberry Wine Jelly

FRUIT SALADS

A fruit salad should be fresh, light and attractively appetizing in appearance. Use best quality fruits, preferably freshly picked.

Some fruits have a particular affinity with each other. For example, the flavour of strawberries and blackcurrants is enhanced by orange; pawpaw tastes quite exotic mixed with lime. Rose water and orange flower water impart a subtle scented flavour to most fruits. Liqueurs improve the flavour of fruits enormously, especially those with a fruity base such as Cointreau and Grand Marnier. If you are lucky enough to have a bottle of Framboise or Kirsch, these liqueurs blend well with any red fruit.

RASPBERRY WINE JELLY

250 g (8 oz) raspberries
3 tablespoons brandy
300 ml (½ pint) water
2 tablespoons gelatine
thinly pared rind and juice of 1 orange
50 g (2 oz) caster sugar
250 ml (8 fl oz) port
4 tablespoons whipping cream, whipped, to decorate

Reserve 6 raspberries for decoration. Divide the remainder between 6 wine glasses. Pour a little brandy into each glass and leave for 1 hour.

Pour a little of the water into a small bowl, sprinkle with the gelatine and soak for 5 minutes. Place the remaining water in a pan with the orange rind and sugar. Heat gently to dissolve the sugar then bring to the boil.

Remove from the heat, add the soaked gelatine and stir until dissolved. Add the orange juice and port and allow to cool.

Strain the wine mixture into the glasses and chill until set.

Decorate each with a rosette of cream and the remaining raspberries.
Serves 6

Melon, Grape and Kiwi Fruit Salad; Summer Salad

FRAISES PLOUGASTEL

This tempting summer dessert is named after the little town of Plougastel in Brittany, which is famous for its excellent strawberries.

*500 g (1 lb)
   strawberries
2 tablespoons caster
   sugar
grated rind and juice
   of ½ orange
2 tablespoons Grand
   Marnier*

Divide half the strawberries between 4 individual serving dishes.

   Place the remaining strawberries in a bowl with the sugar and orange rind, then mash to a pulp using a fork. Add the orange juice and liqueur and mix thoroughly. Pour this pulped mixture over the whole strawberries. Chill in the refrigerator until required.

   Serve with whipped cream.
Serves 4

BLACKCURRANTS AND REDCURRANTS IN COINTREAU

Macerating (or soaking) the fruit in a Cointreau-flavoured syrup softens its texture and improves the flavour – so prepare this delicious fruit salad the day before you intend to serve it.

*grated rind and juice
   of 1 orange
2 tablespoons clear
   honey
3 tablespoons
   Cointreau
250 g (8 oz) red-
   currants
250 g (8 oz) black-
   currants*

Mix together the orange rind and juice, honey and Cointreau. Place the redcurrants and blackcurrants in a serving bowl, pour over the orange-flavoured syrup and chill in the refrigerator overnight.

   Serve with whipped cream.
Serves 4

WATERMELON AND GRAPE COMPOTE

1 small watermelon
250 g (8 oz) black
    grapes, halved and
    seeded
juice of 1 lemon
2 tablespoons clear
    honey
3-4 tablespoons
    orange Curaçao
mint sprigs to decorate

Cut the watermelon into quarters. Cut out the flesh, discard the seeds and cut the watermelon into cubes. Place in a bowl with the grapes. Combine the lemon juice, honey and Curaçao. Pour over the fruit and leave for 1 hour; stir occasionally.

Spoon into individual glass dishes and decorate with mint sprigs to serve.

Serves 6

APRICOT AND ORANGE CREAM

250 g (8 oz) dried
    apricots, roughly
    chopped
300 ml (½ pint)
    orange juice
2 bananas
2 tablespoons Grand
    Marnier
1 orange
142 ml (5 fl oz)
    double cream
2 teaspoons clear
    honey
150 g (5.2 oz)
    natural yogurt

Place the apricots and orange juice in a bowl and leave to soak overnight.

Slice the bananas and add to the bowl with the Grand Marnier. Mix well, then transfer to a glass bowl.

Using a potato peeler, take the rind off half the orange, cut into fine strips and set aside. Grate the remaining rind and mix with the juice of half the orange. Stir this into the cream with the honey, then whip until it stands in stiff peaks. Stir in the yogurt.

Spoon over the fruit and sprinkle with the orange rind strips to serve.

Serves 6

DATE AND ORANGE SALAD

4 oranges
175 g (6 oz) fresh
    dates, stoned
2 tablespoons
    Cointreau
15 g (½ oz) flaked
    almonds, toasted

Peel the oranges, removing all pith, and break into segments over a bowl to catch the juice. Place in the bowl with the dates and Cointreau and mix together. Sprinkle with the almonds to serve.

Serves 4

OPPOSITE: *Fraises Plougastel; Blackcurrants and Redcurrants in Cointreau*
RIGHT: *Watermelon and Grape Compote; Apricot and Orange Cream; Date and Orange Salad*

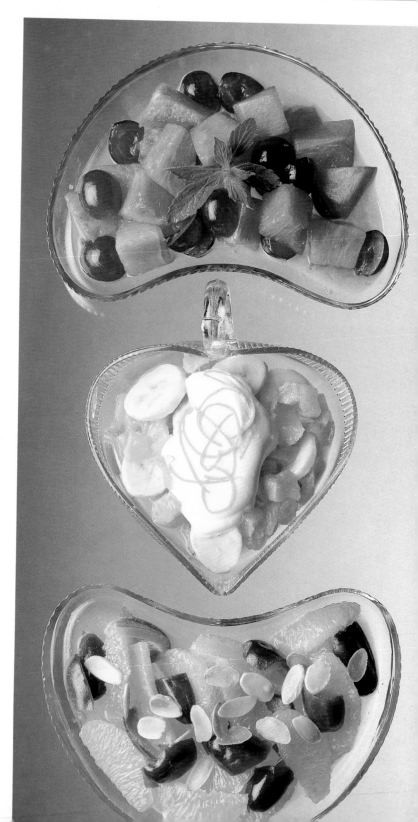

GREEN FRUIT SALAD

150 ml (¼ pint)
   apple juice
1 tablespoon clear
   honey
3 tablespoons kirsch
   or Chartreuse
1 green dessert apple,
   quartered and cored
1 pear, quartered and
   cored
1 Honeydew melon,
   halved and seeded
125 g (4 oz) seedless
   grapes
2 kiwi fruit, peeled
   and sliced
few lemon balm
   leaves, chopped

Mix the apple juice, honey and kirsch or Chartreuse together in a bowl. Slice the apple and pear thinly into the juice and stir to coat completely. Cut the melon flesh into cubes, add to the bowl with the grapes and kiwi fruit and leave for 1 hour, stirring occasionally.

Turn into a serving dish and sprinkle with the lemon balm to serve.

Serves 4 to 6

RASPBERRY CHANTILLY

142 ml (5 fl oz)
   double cream
142 ml (5 fl oz)
   soured cream
1 tablespoon icing
   sugar, sifted
½ teaspoon vanilla
   essence
250 g (8 oz)
   raspberries

Place the two creams together in a bowl with the icing sugar and vanilla essence and whip until it forms soft peaks. Reserve 4 raspberries for decoration. Fold the rest into the cream. Spoon into individual glasses, decorate each with a raspberry and chill. Serve with Nutty Curls or in Lace Baskets (see page 148).

Serves 4

WATERMELON WITH HONEY

1 small watermelon
2 tablespoons clear
   honey
juice of ½ lemon
2 tablespoons sherry
25 g (1 oz) flaked
   almonds, roasted

Scoop the flesh out of the watermelon, discarding the seeds, and cut into cubes.

Mix together the honey, lemon juice and sherry then fold in the melon. Chill for 1 hour.

Spoon into glasses and sprinkle with the almonds to serve.

Serves 4

TIPSY ORANGE SALAD

6 large juicy oranges
2 tablespoons gin
125 g (4 oz) sugar

Pare the rind from one orange and cut into thin shreds. Peel the remaining oranges and remove the white pith from all six. Slice the oranges and put into a serving bowl. Sprinkle over the gin.

Put the sugar and shredded rind into a saucepan and heat gently, stirring until the sugar has melted. Continue heating until the syrup is golden brown and begins to bubble, then pour quickly over the oranges.

Leave for 30 minutes, then chill. Serve with single cream.

Serves 6

LEFT: *Green Fruit Salad*
OPPOSITE: *Strawberry Cassis; Port and Cherry Compote; Strawberries with Yogurt Snow*

STRAWBERRY CASSIS

350 g (12 oz)
  blackcurrants
75 g (3 oz) caster
  sugar
120 ml (4 fl oz)
  water
2 tablespoons orange
  flower water
  (optional)
500 g (1 lb)
  strawberries

Put the blackcurrants, sugar and water in a pan and cook gently, stirring occasionally, until soft. Sieve, pressing as much pulp through as possible. Add the orange flower water if using, and leave to cool.

Place the strawberries in individual bowls, pour over the blackcurrant sauce and chill. Serve with whipped cream.
Serves 6

PORT AND CHERRY COMPOTE

750 g (1½ lb)
  cherries, stoned
2 tablespoons
  redcurrant jelly
120 ml (4 fl oz) port
thinly pared rind and
  juice of 1 orange
2 teaspoons
  arrowroot

Place the cherries in a pan with the redcurrant jelly, port and orange rind. Cover and bring slowly to the boil. Stir gently and simmer for 4 to 5 minutes. Transfer the cherries to individual glass bowls with a slotted spoon. Remove the orange rind.

Blend the orange juice with the arrowroot, then add to the syrup in the pan. Bring to the boil, stirring, and simmer for 1 minute. Cool, then pour over the cherries. Serve with whipped cream.
Serves 4

STRAWBERRIES WITH YOGURT SNOW

150 g (5.2 oz)
  natural yogurt
1 teaspoon lemon
  juice
1 tablespoon brandy
1 egg white
40 g (1½ oz) caster
  sugar
500 g (1 lb)
  strawberries

Mix the yogurt, lemon juice and brandy together. Whisk the egg white until stiff then whisk in the sugar. Fold in the yogurt mixture.

Place the strawberries in individual glass bowls. Spoon the yogurt snow over the strawberries and serve immediately.
Serves 4

SPRING FRUIT SALAD

2 tablespoons clear
    honey
120 ml (4 fl oz)
    water
thinly pared rind and
    juice of 1 lemon
1 red dessert apple,
    quartered and cored
1 pear, quartered and
    cored
1 banana
1 small pineapple
2 oranges
125 g (4 oz) black
    grapes, halved and
    seeded
125 g (4 oz)
    strawberries, sliced

Place the honey, water and lemon rind in a small pan. Bring to the boil, simmer for 2 minutes, then strain and leave to cool. Stir in the lemon juice.

Slice the apple, pear and banana into a bowl, pour over the lemon syrup and stir to coat the fruit completely.

Peel the pineapple with a sharp knife and cut the flesh into sections, discarding the central core.

Peel the oranges, removing all pith, and divide into segments. Add to the bowl with the pineapple, grapes and strawberries and mix well.

Turn into a glass dish and chill until required. Serve with whipped cream.
Serves 8

Spring Fruit Salad

SUNSET FRUIT SALAD

1 Ogen melon
250 g (8 oz) grapes
250 g (8 oz)
    strawberries
grated rind and juice
    of 1 orange
1 tablespoon sherry
1 teaspoon caster
    sugar
½ teaspoon ground
    ginger
150 g (5 oz) natural
    low-fat yogurt
4 pieces preserved
    ginger to decorate

Peel the melon and cut into cubes. Cut the grapes in half and remove the pips. Wash and hull the strawberries and cut into slices. Place all the fruit in a bowl.

Mix together the orange rind, juice, sherry, sugar and ground ginger. Pour over the fruit and leave to soak for several hours, stirring occasionally.

Spoon the fruit into glass serving dishes, top with the yogurt and decorate with preserved ginger.
Serves 4
NOTE: This makes an excellent low calorie dessert for slimmers. Each portion has approximately 120 calories (500 KJ).

CARIBBEAN SALAD

1 Charentais or
    Galia melon,
    halved and seeded
1 mango, peeled
1 banana
3 tablespoons white
    rum
lemon balm sprigs to
    decorate (optional)

Cut the flesh out of the melon halves and cut into slices. Reserve the shells.

Cut the mango in half lengthways, as close to the stone as possible. Using a sharp knife, remove the stone. Cut the flesh into slices and place in a bowl with the melon.

Slice the banana and add to the fruit with the rum. Stir well, then spoon into the reserved melon shells and decorate with lemon balm if using.
Serves 4 to 6

TROPICAL FRUITS

Tropical fruits provide an exciting alternative to the more familiar ingredients used in fruit salads. They are becoming more widely available in larger supermarkets and good food stores. Spring is a particularly good time to buy them – when home-produced fruits are in limited supply.

Look out for the more unusual tropical fruits, such as passion fruit, pawpaw, mango and guava. They are absolutely delicious and well worth trying. Passion fruit goes particularly well with banana – a more common tropical fruit. It is traditionally included in Pavlova (see page 83).

POLYNESIAN PAWPAW SALAD

Pawpaw is also known as papaya. It has a delicious pinkish orange flesh enclosed in a yellow and green freckled skin. Pawpaw are ready to eat when they yield to gentle pressure applied in the palm of your hand. They are delicious served simply sprinkled with lime juice.

1 pawpaw
juice of ½ lime
1 pink-fleshed grapefruit
lime slices to decorate

Cut the pawpaw into quarters and remove the seeds. Peel and slice into a glass bowl. Pour over the lime juice.

Peel the grapefruit, removing all pith, and cut into segments. Add to the bowl and chill until required.

Decorate with lime slices to serve.
Serves 4

TROPICAL FRUIT SALAD

1 small pineapple
1 × 312 g (11 oz) can lychees, drained
2 bananas, sliced
1 × 411 g (14½ oz) can guavas, drained and sliced
2 passion fruit (optional)
250 ml (8 fl oz) ginger ale

Cut the pineapple in half lengthways, remove the flesh and cut into pieces, discarding the centre core. Place in a bowl with the lychees, bananas and guavas.

Halve the passion fruit if using, scoop out the flesh and mix with the other fruits. Pour over the ginger ale and chill. Serve with cream if liked.
Serves 8

GUAVA PASSION

2 oranges
1 × 411 g (14½ oz) can guavas
2 bananas (optional)
125 g (4 oz) black grapes, halved and seeded
2 passion fruit

Peel the oranges, removing all pith, and cut into segments.

Place the oranges in a serving bowl with the juice from the guavas. Slice the guavas and bananas if using, and add to the bowl with the grapes.

Halve the passion fruit, scoop out the flesh and mix with the other fruit. Serve with whipped cream.
Serves 6

Polynesian Pawpaw Salad; Caribbean Salad; Guava Passion

DRIED FRUIT AND MELON COMPOTE

15 dried figs, chopped
15 dried dates, stoned and chopped
50 g (2 oz) blanched hazelnuts
50 g (2 oz) blanched almonds
175 g (6 oz) clear honey
6 tablespoons Kirsch
1 large honeydew melon, halved and seeded

Mix together the figs, dates, nuts, honey and Kirsch in a serving dish. Leave to soak for 3 hours, stirring occasionally.

Cut the melon flesh into balls using a melon baller, or cut into cubes. Add to the fruit mixture and stir well. Chill for about 1 hour before serving, with single cream.
Serves 6

DATE AND APRICOT SALAD

175 g (6 oz) dried apricots
300 ml (½ pint) water
120 ml (4 fl oz) apple juice
125 g (4 oz) fresh dates
2 bananas

Soak the apricots in the water for 2 hours, then cook gently for 10 minutes. Pour into a serving bowl with the apple juice and dates and allow to cool.

Slice the bananas into the bowl and mix well. Chill until required. Serve with cream.
Serves 4

APRICOT JELLY

250 g (8 oz) dried apricots, soaked overnight
juice of ½ lemon
1-2 tablespoons clear honey
15 g (½ oz) gelatine, soaked in 3 tablespoons water

Place the apricots in a pan with the liquid in which they were soaked, adding more water if necessary to cover. Simmer for 20 to 30 minutes until tender.

Place the apricots and liquid in an electric blender with the lemon juice and honey and blend until smooth. Add water to make up to 750 ml (1¼ pints) if necessary.

Place the soaked gelatine in a bowl over a pan of simmering water and stir until dissolved. Stir into the apricot mixture.

Pour into a 900 ml (1½ pint) ring mould and chill until set.

Dip the mould quickly into hot water to loosen and turn out onto a serving dish.
Serves 4 to 6

DRIED FRUITS

Although summer is naturally the best time for fruit salads, some excellent recipes can be created in winter. With so many dried fruits and imported citrus fruits available it is possible to make a tempting fruit salad at any time of the year. Of the most commonly available dried fruits – dates, figs, apricots, apples and prunes (dried plums) are the most suitable for fruit salads. Look out for less common varieties – such as pears and peaches – to ring the changes.

Dried apricots, figs and prunes should be washed, then soaked for several hours or overnight (according to the recipe). Dried fruits should be cooked, where possible, in their soaking liquor to retain flavour and nutrients.

LEFT: *Apricot Jelly*
OPPOSITE: *Winter Fruit Salad; Fruit Chartreuse*

WINTER FRUIT SALAD

600 ml (1 pint)
 water
2 tablespoons clear
 honey
2.5 cm (1 inch) piece
 of cinnamon stick
2 cloves
juice of ½ lemon
175 g (6 oz) dried
 apricots, soaked
 overnight
125 g (4 oz) dried
 prunes, soaked
 overnight
125 g (4 oz) dried
 figs, soaked
 overnight
50 g (2 oz) raisins
25 g (1 oz) walnut
 halves, coarsely
 chopped
25 g (1 oz) flaked
 almonds, toasted

Place the water, honey, cinnamon and cloves in a pan and bring to the boil. Add the lemon juice. Drain the dried fruits and add to the pan. Cover and simmer gently for 10 minutes.

Add the raisins and simmer for 2 to 3 minutes. Discard the cinnamon and cloves.

Spoon into individual serving dishes and sprinkle with the walnuts and almonds. Serve hot or cold, with cream if liked.

Serves 6

FRUIT CHARTREUSE

900 ml (1½ pints)
 water
200 g (7 oz) sugar
thinly pared rind and
 juice of 3 lemons
2.5 cm (1 inch) piece
 of cinnamon stick
40 g (1½ oz)
 gelatine
4 tablespoons sherry
175 g (6 oz) black
 grapes, seeded
175 g (6 oz) green
 grapes, seeded
142 ml (5 fl oz)
 double cream,
 whipped

Put 750 ml (1¼ pints) of the water, the sugar, lemon rind, juice and cinnamon stick in a pan. Heat gently, stirring, until the sugar is dissolved.

Add the gelatine to the remaining water. Leave to soak for 5 minutes, then add to the lemon mixture and heat gently, stirring, until dissolved. Add the sherry and allow to cool slightly. Discard the cinnamon.

Pour a little of the mixture into a 1.2 litre (2 pint) ring mould and chill in the refrigerator until set. Arrange some black grapes on the surface, pour on just enough jelly to cover and leave to set. Add another layer of jelly, leave to set, then arrange green grapes on top. Continue in this way until the mould is full; chill until set.

Turn out onto a serving dish and decorate with piped cream and any remaining grapes.

Serves 6 to 8

BANANAS BAKED WITH RUM AND ALMONDS

8 large bananas
1 tablespoon sugar
120 ml (4 fl oz)
white rum
284 ml (10 fl oz)
double cream
250 g (8 oz)
macaroons, crushed
25 g (1 oz) blanched
almonds, chopped
15 g (½ oz) butter,
melted

Cut the bananas in half lengthways, then each half in half crossways. Place the pieces in a baking dish and sprinkle with sugar and rum. Bake in a preheated moderate oven, 160°C (325°F), Gas Mark 3, for 15 minutes.

Pour the cream over the bananas. Mix together the macaroons and almonds and sprinkle over the top. Drizzle with the butter.

Return to the oven and bake for 20 minutes. Serve hot.

Serves 6 to 8

NOTE: If you wish to make the macaroons, see page 150.

MIXED FRUIT BRÛLÉE

3 tablespoons sugar
(or to taste)
6 tablespoons water
1 tablespoon lemon
juice
750 g-1 kg (1½-2 lb)
mixed fruit in
season
(strawberries,
peaches, bananas,
apples, pears,
grapes, etc.), cored
and sliced as
necessary
284 ml (10 fl oz)
double cream
4 tablespoons dark
brown sugar

Dissolve the sugar in the water in a small saucepan. Stir in the lemon juice and remove from the heat.

Put the prepared fruit into a flameproof serving dish and stir in the sugar syrup. Press the fruit down to level the top. Whip the cream until stiff and spread over the fruit. Chill until just before serving.

To serve, sprinkle the cream with the brown sugar and grill until the sugar melts. Serve immediately.

Serves 4 to 6

PÊCHES BRÛLÉES

6 fresh peaches,
  skinned
2 tablespoons
  Cointreau
284 ml (10 fl oz)
  double cream,
  whipped
125 g (4 oz) soft
  brown sugar

Halve the peaches, discard the stones and place in a shallow ovenproof dish. Pour over the Cointreau.

Spread the cream over the peaches to cover them completely and sprinkle with the sugar. Place under a preheated hot grill for 3 minutes or until the sugar has caramelized.

Cool, then chill before serving.
Serves 6

STRAWBERRY BRÛLÉE

250 g (8 oz)
  strawberries,
  halved
2 tablespoons Grand
  Marnier or kirsch
284 ml (10 fl oz)
  double cream,
  whipped
125 g (4 oz) soft
  brown sugar

Place the strawberries in 6 ramekins and sprinkle with the liqueur. Divide the cream between the ramekins, smoothing to the edges. Cover, seal and freeze for 30 minutes.

Sprinkle with the sugar and place under a preheated hot grill for 1 minute or until the sugar has caramelized.

Cool and chill before serving.
Serves 6

CARIBBEAN BANANAS

4 bananas, halved
  lengthways
75 g (3 oz) soft
  brown sugar
2 tablespoons lemon
  juice
25 g (1 oz) butter
2 tablespoons rum

Place the bananas in an ovenproof dish and sprinkle with the sugar and lemon juice. Dot with the butter and bake in a preheated moderate oven, 180°C (350°F), Gas Mark 4, for 15 minutes.

Arrange the bananas in a warmed serving dish and spoon over the cooking liquor.

Warm the rum in a ladle, ignite and pour over the bananas. Serve flaming, with cream if liked.
Serves 4

OPPOSITE: *Bananas Baked with Rum and Almonds; Mixed Fruit Brûlée*
RIGHT: *Hot Fruit Salad*

HOT FRUIT SALAD

175 g (6 oz) dried
  apricots
125 g (4 oz) dried
  prunes
125 g (4 oz) dried
  figs
125 g (4 oz) dried
  apples
600 ml (1 pint) apple
  juice
2 tablespoons
  Calvados
  or brandy
25 g (1 oz) walnuts,
  coarsely chopped

Place the dried fruits in a bowl with the apple juice and leave to soak overnight.

Transfer to a saucepan and simmer for 10 to 15 minutes. Turn into a glass bowl and pour over the Calvados or brandy. Sprinkle with the walnuts. Serve immediately with natural low-fat yogurt.
Serves 6
NOTE: This healthy fruit salad can alternatively be made in advance and served cold. Other dried fruit, such as peaches, pears and dates, can be included if liked.

CALVADOS APPLES

125 g (4 oz) sugar
300 ml (½ pint)
  water
6 dessert apples,
  peeled and
  quartered
3 tablespoons
  Calvados or
  brandy
CARAMEL:
75 g (3 oz) sugar
3 tablespoons water
TO SERVE:
Brandy Snaps (see
  page 148)

Place the sugar and water in a pan and heat gently, stirring, until dissolved. Bring to the boil, then simmer for 5 minutes. Place the apples in the syrup, cover and simmer gently for 15 to 20 minutes until the apples look clear. Leave to cool in the syrup, then transfer the apples to a glass serving dish.

Boil the syrup rapidly until reduced by about half, then add the Calvados or brandy. Pour over the apples. Leave to cool.

To make the caramel: Place the sugar and water in a pan and heat gently, stirring, until dissolved, then boil rapidly until golden brown. Pour onto an oiled baking sheet and leave to harden. When set, crack the caramel into pieces and sprinkle over the apples.

Serve with brandy snaps and whipped cream.
Serves 4

RED FRUIT COMPOTE

250 g (8 oz) sugar
300 ml (½ pint)
  water
500 g (1 lb)
  blackcurrants
grated rind and juice
  of ½ orange
125 g (4 oz)
  strawberries
125 g (4 oz)
  blackberries
250 g (8 oz)
  raspberries
1 tablespoon
  arrowroot
2 tablespoons port
Crémets (see right) to
  serve

Place the sugar and water in a pan and heat gently, stirring, until dissolved. Bring to the boil and boil for a few minutes, then add the blackcurrants and orange rind. Simmer gently for 15 minutes until soft.

Strain the fruit, reserving the syrup. Place the blackcurrants in a serving dish and add the remaining fruit.

Return the syrup to the pan and bring to the boil. Mix the arrowroot with the orange juice and stir into the boiling syrup. Cook, stirring, until thickened and clear. Add the port and pour the syrup over the fruit. Allow to cool. Chill before serving, with crémets.
Serves 8

RASPBERRY AND HAZELNUT CRUNCH

75 g (3 oz)
  margarine or butter
125 g (4 oz) wholemeal
  breadcrumbs
75 g (3 oz)
  muscovado sugar
50 g (2 oz) hazelnuts,
  chopped and roasted
350 g (12 oz)
  raspberries

Melt the margarine or butter in a frying pan, add the breadcrumbs and cook until golden. Cool, then stir in the sugar and hazelnuts.

Set aside 4 raspberries. Divide half the remainder between individual glass dishes and cover with half the crumbs; repeat the layers.

Top with the raspberries and serve chilled, with natural low-fat yogurt.
Serves 4

RASPBERRY CHEESE DESSERT

750 g (1½ lb) fresh
  or frozen
  raspberries, thawed
75 g (3 oz) caster
  sugar
grated rind of 1 lemon
500 g (1 lb) skimmed
  milk soft cheese
4 tablespoons brandy
  or raspberry
  liqueur
6 mint sprigs

Place the raspberries in an electric blender or food processor with the sugar and lemon rind and work to a purée. Set half on one side.

Add half of the cheese and brandy or liqueur to the purée in the blender or processor and process until smooth. Transfer to 3 individual glass dishes. Repeat with the remaining ingredients.

Garnish with the mint leaves to serve.
Serves 6

CRÉMETS

175 g (6 oz) curd
  cheese
1 tablespoon caster
  sugar
170 ml (6 fl oz)
  double cream

Mix the cheese with the sugar, then gradually beat in the cream. Pile into a serving dish and chill. Serve with stewed fruit.
Serves 4 to 6

Red Fruit Compote; Calvados Apples; Crémets

BANANA SPLITS

4 bananas
juice of ½ lemon
1 × 75 g (3 oz) bar
*   milk chocolate,*
*   coarsely grated*
TOPPING:
whipped cream or
*   vanilla ice cream*
chopped walnuts
*   (optional)*

Peel the bananas and split lengthwise without cutting right through. Sprinkle with lemon juice. Spoon the grated chocolate into the banana splits. Wrap each banana separately in foil and place on a baking sheet.

Cook in a preheated moderate oven, 180°C (350°F), Gas Mark 4, for 20 minutes. Unwrap and serve the bananas topped with whipped cream or vanilla ice cream and chopped walnuts, if liked.
Serves 4

APRICOT YOGURT DESSERT

300 g (10 oz) natural
*   yogurt*
juice of ½ orange
1-2 tablespoons clear
*   honey*
125 g (4 oz) dried
*   apricots, chopped*

Place the yogurt in a bowl with the orange juice, honey and apricots. Leave in the refrigerator overnight.

Spoon the dessert into individual glasses and serve with Almond Curls (see page 151).
Serves 4 to 6

PEACHES IN BLACKCURRANT SAUCE

500 g (1 lb)
*   blackcurrants*
125 g (4 oz) caster
*   sugar*
250 ml (8 fl oz)
*   water*
grated rind and juice
*   of 1 orange*
6 ripe peaches, peeled

Put the blackcurrants, sugar and water in a pan and cook gently, stirring occasionally, until soft. Sieve, pressing as much pulp through as possible. Add the orange rind and juice.

Place the peaches in a serving bowl and pour over the blackcurrant purée. Chill and serve with cream if liked.
Serves 6

QUICK DESSERTS

Most of the recipes in this chapter are straightforward, but the desserts on this page are particularly quick and easy to prepare. It only takes a few minutes to assemble a banana split and this is always a popular dish with children.

A light yogurt dessert – such as the one above – is the ideal way to round off many meals. It is also, of course, an excellent choice for slimmers. Always keep a large tub of natural yogurt in the refrigerator for those occasions when you haven't the time or energy to prepare any other kind of pudding. A portion of natural yogurt – sweetened with a little clear honey if liked – can be served in a multitude of different ways. Serve it combined with chopped fruit, such as pineapple, or fresh soft fruits in season, such as strawberries, blackberries or raspberries; mixed with a fruit purée; or topped with a light sprinkling of muesli and chopped nuts.

LEFT: *Peaches in Blackcurrant Sauce*
OPPOSITE: *Pears in Red Wine; Oranges in Caramel*

PEARS IN RED WINE

150 g (5 oz) sugar
150 ml (¼ pint)
    water
150 ml (¼ pint) red
    wine
2.5 cm (1 inch) piece
    of cinnamon stick
6 dessert pears
2 teaspoons arrowroot

Place the sugar, water, wine and cinnamon in a pan. Heat gently until the sugar is dissolved. Bring to the boil and boil for 5 minutes.

Peel the pears, leaving on the stalks, and place in the prepared syrup. Cover and simmer gently for 20 to 30 minutes until translucent. Discard the cinnamon stick. Arrange the pears on a serving dish.

Mix the arrowroot with a little water, then add to the syrup and bring to the boil, stirring. Simmer, stirring, for 1 minute until clear. Leave to cool. Spoon over the pears and chill. Serve with whipped cream.
Serves 6

ORANGES IN CARAMEL

8 small oranges
250 g (8 oz) sugar
120 ml (4 fl oz) cold
    water
150 ml (¼ pint) hot
    water
Brandy Snaps (see
    page 148) to serve

Pare the rind from 1 orange and shred finely. Cook in boiling water for 1 minute, then drain and dry.

Peel the oranges, removing all the pith. Cut into thin slices and hold together with cocktail sticks. Arrange in individual dishes.

Place the sugar and cold water in a pan. Heat gently until dissolved, then boil steadily to a rich brown caramel. Carefully add the hot water and stir until the caramel has melted, heating again if necessary. Leave to cool.

Pour the caramel over the oranges, top with the shredded rind and chill. Serve with brandy snaps.
Serves 4

FIGGY APPLES

4 large cooking
    apples, cored
1 tablespoon clear
    honey
75 g (3 oz) dried figs,
    chopped
1 tablespoon lemon
    juice
4 tablespoons apple
    juice

Make a shallow cut round the middle of each apple.

Place the honey, figs and lemon juice in a small pan and heat gently, stirring, until mixed. Use to fill the apple cavities, pressing the mixture down firmly.

Place in an ovenproof dish and pour over the apple juice. Bake in a preheated moderate oven, 180°C (350°F), Gas Mark 4, for 45 to 55 minutes until soft. Serve hot with natural yogurt or single cream.
Serves 4

Figgy Apples

BAKED APPLES WITH DATES

4 large cooking
    apples
50 g (2 oz) dates,
    stoned and chopped
25 g (1 oz) raisins
25 g (1 oz) soft
    brown sugar
½ teaspoon ground
    cinnamon
4 tablespoons cider

Remove the cores from the apples. Make a shallow cut round the middle of each one.

Mix together the dates, raisins, sugar and cinnamon and use to fill the apple cavities, pressing down firmly.

Place in an ovenproof dish and add the cider. Bake in a preheated moderate oven, 180°C (350°F), Gas Mark 4, for 50 minutes, or until soft. Serve hot with cream or custard.
Serves 4

AUTUMN PUDDING

500 g (1 lb) cooking
    apples, peeled,
    cored and sliced
375 g (12 oz)
    blackberries
50 g (2 oz) soft
    brown sugar
2 tablespoons water
3 tablespoons port
8 slices brown bread,
    crusts removed

Place the apples, blackberries and sugar in a heavy-based pan with the water. Cover and simmer gently until soft but not pulpy. Add the port and leave to cool. Strain, reserving the juice.

Cut 3 circles of bread to fit the base, middle and top of a 900 ml (1½ pint) pudding basin. Shape the remaining bread to fit around the side of the basin.

Soak the bread in the reserved fruit juice as you line the basin. Start with the small circle in the bottom of the basin, then the shaped bread round the side. Spoon in half the fruit and place the middle-sized circle of bread on top. Cover with the remaining fruit then top with the large bread circle. Fold over any bread protruding over the top of the basin. Cover with a saucer small enough to fit inside the basin and put a 500 g (1 lb) weight on top. Leave in the refrigerator overnight.

Turn onto a serving plate, pour over any remaining fruit juice and serve with whipped cream.
Serves 6 to 8

APPLE AND BLACKBERRY FOOL

500 g (1 lb) cooking
  apples, peeled,
  cored and sliced
250 g (8 oz)
  blackberries
50 g (2 oz) soft
  brown sugar
284 ml (10 fl oz)
  double cream,
  whipped

Place the apples, blackberries and sugar in a heavy-based pan. Cover and simmer gently for 15 minutes, until soft. Allow to cool, then work in an electric blender or food processor to make a purée. Sieve to remove the pips.

Fold the cream into the purée. Spoon into individual dishes and chill. Serve with Cigarettes Russes (see page 149).
Serves 6

BLACKCURRANT SUEDOISE

MERINGUE:
2 egg whites
125 g (4 oz) caster
  sugar
FRUIT JELLY:
125 g (4 oz) sugar
150 ml (¼ pint)
  water
500 g (1 lb)
  blackcurrants
20 g (¾ oz) gelatine,
  soaked in
  4 tablespoons cold
  water
142 ml (5 fl oz)
  double cream,
  whipped
1 teaspoon grated
  chocolate

Whisk the egg whites until stiff, then whisk in 3 tablespoons of the sugar. Carefully fold in the remaining sugar.

Put the meringue into a piping bag, fitted with a 5 mm (¼ inch) plain nozzle and pipe tiny mounds onto a baking sheet lined with silicone paper. Bake in a preheated cool oven, 150°C (300°F), Gas Mark 2, for 1½ to 2 hours.

Place the sugar and water in a pan. Heat, stirring, until dissolved. Add the blackcurrants and cook gently for 15 minutes. Purée in an electric blender or rub through a sieve.

Place the soaked gelatine in a bowl over a pan of simmering water and stir until dissolved. Add to the purée and leave until beginning to set, stirring occasionally. Pour into a dampened 18 cm (7 inch) soufflé dish and leave in the refrigerator to set.

Turn out onto a plate. Spread the cream over the suedoise and top with meringues. Sprinkle with chocolate.
Serves 6

Apple and Blackberry Fool; Autumn Pudding

SUMMER PUDDING

*500 g (1 lb) mixed
redcurrants,
blackcurrants and
blackberries*
*125 g (4 oz) caster
sugar*
*250 g (8 oz)
raspberries*
*8 slices white bread,
crusts removed*
*whipped cream or
Crémets (see page
20) to serve*

Place the currants and blackberries in a heavy pan with the sugar. Cook gently, stirring occasionally, for 10 to 15 minutes until tender. Add the raspberries and leave to cool. Strain the fruit, reserving the juice.

Cut 3 circles of bread to fit the base, middle and top of a 900 ml (1½ pint) pudding basin. Shape the remaining bread to fit round the sides of the basin. Soak all the bread in the reserved fruit juice.

Line the bottom of the basin with the small circle, then arrange the shaped bread around the sides. Pour in half the fruit and place another circle of bread on top. Cover with the remaining fruit, then top with the large bread circle.

Cover with a saucer small enough to fit inside the basin and put a 500 g (1 lb) weight on top. Leave in the refrigerator overnight.

Turn onto a serving plate, pour over any remaining fruit juice and serve with whipped cream or crémets.
Serves 8

APPLE SNOW

*500 g (1 lb) cooking
apples, peeled and
cored*
*50 g (2 oz) caster
sugar*
2 tablespoons water
2 egg whites
*grated rind and juice
of ½ lemon*
*Sponge Fingers (see
page 151) to serve*

Slice the apples into a pan, sprinkle with the sugar and add the water. Cover and simmer gently for 10 to 15 minutes, then work in an electric blender until smooth or rub through a sieve. Leave to cool.

Whisk the egg whites until stiff and fold into the apple purée with the lemon rind and juice.

Spoon into glasses and serve with sponge fingers.
Serves 4

Apple Snow; Apple Mould; Summer Pudding

APPLE MOULD

175 g (6 oz) sugar
6 tablespoons water
*grated rind and juice
of 1 lemon*
*1 kg (2 lb) dessert
apples, peeled and
cored*
*50 g (2 oz) glacé
cherries, chopped*
*50 g (2 oz) preserved
ginger, chopped*
YOGURT SAUCE:
*142 ml (5 fl oz)
double cream*
*150 g (5 oz) natural
low-fat yogurt*
*1 tablespoon caster
sugar*

Place the sugar, water, lemon rind and juice in a pan and heat gently, stirring, until dissolved. Bring to the boil and boil for 5 minutes.

Thinly slice the apples into the syrup. Cover and simmer gently for 10 minutes, turning the apples once carefully. Remove the lid and simmer until most of the syrup has evaporated.

Add the cherries and ginger to the pan, cover and leave to cool.

Turn the mixture into a dampened 900 ml (1½ pint) soufflé dish and leave overnight in the refrigerator.

To make the sauce: Whip the cream until it holds its shape then fold in the yogurt and sugar.

Turn the apple mould out onto a serving plate and serve with the yogurt sauce.
Serves 6

FREEZING APPLE PURÉE

Apples are on sale all the year round at reasonable prices and of course many of us have our own home-grown supply in the autumn. For this reason you will find plenty of ideas in this chapter for imaginative apple desserts – alternatives to the ubiquitous apple pie. There are many different varieties of apples to choose from, but for cooking the Bramley is a traditional and excellent choice.

If you are lucky enough to have a glut of apples in the autumn – and a freezer – it is well worth freezing some apples in purée form for later use. Apple purée is ideal for making quick desserts, including some of those featuring apples in this chapter.

To prepare apple purée for the freezer: working in small batches, peel, core and slice the apples, discarding any bruised, decayed or insect-infected areas, then toss slices in lemon juice. Cook gently in the minimum amount of water until soft. Sweeten, if liked, after cooking, but remember that this does limit uses. The mixture can either be left rather lumpy or puréed in an electric blender or food processor until smooth, or passed through a nylon sieve before freezing. Pour into rigid freezerproof containers in usable quantities, leaving a 2 cm (¾ inch) headspace. Seal, label and freeze for up to 8 months.

To thaw: leave to stand in the container at room temperature for 1 to 2 hours. Use in any dessert made with an apple purée.

ICES AND SORBETS

Ice creams are, of course, universally popular with adults and children alike. They also happen to be easy to make and they are infinitely superior in both flavour and composition to bought ices. The only additives in home-made ice cream are those you add yourself! Ice creams can be made with a cream or custard base. The choice of flavourings is endless – coffee, chocolate, ginger, mint, various nuts and all kinds of fruit.

Sorbets are particularly refreshing – ideal for hot summer days. They are lighter and softer than ice creams. Essentially a sorbet is a water ice, flavoured with either fruit or liqueur and stabilized with egg white. Fruit sorbets, such as lemon, orange and pineapple look most attractive served in the hollowed out fruit.

Ideally ices and sorbets should be frozen quickly in the freezer. Satisfactory results can be obtained in the freezing compartment of the refrigerator if it is turned to the coldest setting a few hours before you begin preparation.

To obtain a really smooth textured sorbet or ice cream it is usually necessary to beat the partially frozen mixture thoroughly, at least once. If you plan to make ice cream frequently, it is probably worth investing in an electric operated ice cream maker which churns the mixture during freezing, saving you time and effort.

If you have a freezer, it is a good idea to make extra ice creams and sorbets to store for those unexpected guests. Ices and frozen desserts are probably the most versatile of all desserts – you will find them an excellent way to round off any meal.

PINEAPPLE WATER ICE

1 large pineapple,
  halved lengthwise
175 g (6 oz)
  granulated sugar
450 ml (¾ pint)
  water
1 egg white

Remove the core from the pineapple. Scrape out the flesh and juice; place in an electric blender or food processor and work to a purée. Chill the shells.

Place the sugar and water in a pan and heat gently until dissolved. Boil for 5 minutes, then cool. Add the pineapple pulp and pour into a rigid freezerproof container. Cover, seal and freeze for 3 hours, until half-frozen.

Whisk the egg white until stiff, then gradually whisk in the water ice, until frothy. Cover, seal and freeze until firm.

Transfer to the refrigerator 10 minutes before serving. Scoop into the pineapple shells to serve.
Serves 6 to 8

APRICOT ICE CREAM

350 g (12 oz) dried
  apricots, soaked in
  water for 2 hours
2 tablespoons lemon
  juice
3 egg whites
175 g (6 oz) caster
  sugar
284 ml (10 fl oz)
  double cream,
  whipped

Place the apricots and soaking liquid in a pan, adding enough water to cover. Simmer gently, covered, for 20 minutes. Drain, reserving 150 ml (¼ pint) liquid. Cool slightly, then put the apricots, reserved liquid and lemon juice into an electric blender or food processor and work to a purée. Cool completely.

Whisk the egg whites until stiff, then gradually whisk in the sugar. Fold the cream and apricot purée into the meringue mixture. Turn into a rigid freezerproof container. Cover, seal and freeze until solid.

Transfer to the refrigerator 30 minutes before serving to soften.
Serves 6 to 8

APPLE AND CALVADOS SORBET

750 g (1½ lb) cooking
  apples, peeled,
  cored and sliced
450 ml (¾ pint)
  water
grated rind and juice
  of 1 lemon
175 g (6 oz) sugar
1 egg white
1-2 tablespoons
  Calvados
mint leaves to
  decorate

Place the apples in a pan with 150 ml (¼ pint) of the water. Cover and simmer until soft. Cool slightly, pour into an electric blender or food processor and add the lemon rind and juice. Work to a smooth purée and cool completely.

Heat the remaining water with the sugar, gently until dissolved. Boil for 5 minutes then cool. Add the apple purée, then pour into a rigid freezerproof container. Cover, seal and freeze for 3 hours, until half-frozen.

Whisk the egg white until stiff, then gradually whisk in the water ice, until frothy. Cover, seal and freeze for 2 hours.

Whisk in the Calvados. Cover, seal and re-freeze until firm.

Transfer to the refrigerator 10 minutes before serving. Decorate with mint leaves.
Serves 6 to 8

VANILLA ICE CREAM

2 eggs
2 egg yolks
75 g (3 oz) caster
  sugar
426 ml (15 fl oz)
  single cream
2-3 drops of vanilla
  essence
284 ml (10 fl oz)
  double cream,
  whipped
Langue de Chat
  biscuits (see page
  149) to serve

Mix the eggs, egg yolks and sugar together. Bring the single cream gently to the boil and pour onto the egg mixture, stirring vigorously. Strain, then stir in the vanilla essence. Leave to cool, then fold in the whipped cream.

Pour into a rigid freezerproof container. Cover, seal and freeze for 1 hour. Remove and stir well, then re-freeze until firm.

Transfer to the refrigerator 20 minutes before serving to soften. Scoop into chilled glasses and serve with langue de chat or wafer biscuits.

Serves 8

VARIATIONS:

Chocolate: Break 250 g (8 oz) plain chocolate into pieces and melt with the single cream.

Praline: Place 50 g (2 oz) blanched almonds and 50 g (2 oz) caster sugar in a pan and heat gently until the sugar melts. Cook, stirring, until nut brown. Turn onto an oiled baking sheet and leave until hard. Crush with a rolling pin and add to the custard with the double cream.

Coffee: Dissolve 3 tablespoons instant coffee powder in 2 tablespoons boiling water, cool and add to the custard with the double cream.

Ginger: Finely chop 125 g (4 oz) preserved stem ginger. Add to the eggs and sugar. Add 2 tablespoons of the ginger syrup to the custard with the double cream.

BANANA ICE

1 × 426 ml (¾ pint)
  can evaporated
  milk, chilled
125 g (4 oz) soft
  brown sugar
3 ripe bananas
1 tablespoon lemon
  juice
wafer biscuits to
  serve

Whisk the evaporated milk until thick and mousse-like, using an electric beater if possible, then whisk in the sugar. Mash the bananas to a pulp with the lemon juice, then whisk into the evaporated milk.

Turn into a rigid freezerproof container. Cover and freeze for 1 hour. Stir well, then re-freeze until firm.

Transfer to the refrigerator 30 minutes before serving to soften. Scoop into chilled glasses and serve with wafer biscuits.

Serves 8

OPPOSITE: *Apple and Calvados Sorbet; Pineapple Water Ice; Apricot Ice Cream*
RIGHT: *Chocolate Ice Cream; Ginger Ice Cream; Vanilla Ice Cream; Praline Ice Cream; Banana Ice; Coffee Ice Cream*

ORANGE ICE CREAM

4 large oranges
4 egg yolks
125 g (4 oz) caster
 sugar
284 ml (10 fl oz)
 single cream
142 ml (5 fl oz)
 double cream,
 whipped
6-8 chocolate
 triangles (see page
 123) to decorate

Halve two of the oranges, carefully scoop out the flesh and juice and sieve to extract all juices; keep on one side. Freeze the orange shells.

Finely grate the rind of the remaining oranges and place in a heatproof bowl with the egg yolks and sugar. Beat until thoroughly blended. Heat the single cream to just below boiling point; stir into the egg yolk mixture. Place the bowl over a pan of simmering water and stir until thickened. Add the orange juice, strain and cool.

Fold the orange custard into the double cream and turn into a rigid freezerproof container. Cover, seal and freeze until firm.

Scoop into the reserved orange shells, piling up well. Return the leftover ice cream to the freezer for another occasion or scoop into extra shells or individual glasses.

Decorate each with a chocolate triangle and serve immediately, or return to the freezer until required.
Serves 6 to 8

ORANGE SORBET

450 ml (¾ pint)
 water
75 g (3 oz) sugar
thinly pared rind and
 juice of 1 lemon
184 g (6½ oz) can
 frozen concentrated
 orange juice,
 thawed
1 egg white

Place the water, sugar, lemon rind and juice in a pan and heat gently, stirring until dissolved. Bring to the boil, simmer for 5 minutes, then allow to cool.

Remove the lemon rind and add the orange juice. Turn into a rigid freezerproof container. Cover, seal and freeze.

When half-frozen, whisk the egg white and fold into the sorbet. Return to the freezer; stir once or twice during freezing.

Transfer to the refrigerator 10 minutes before serving to soften. Scoop into chilled glasses.
Serves 6

ST CLEMENT'S ICE CREAM

3 eggs, separated
175 g (6 oz) caster
 sugar
grated rind and juice
 of 1 lemon
grated rind and juice
 of 1 orange
284 ml (10 fl oz)
 double cream,
 whipped

Whisk the egg yolks, half the sugar and the lemon and orange rinds together until thick and creamy. Strain the fruit juices into a pan and heat gently, then pour onto the egg mixture and continue whisking until thick.

Whisk the egg whites until stiff, then whisk in the remaining sugar. Fold into the egg mixture, with the cream.

Turn into a rigid freezerproof container. Cover, seal and freeze until firm.

Scoop into chilled glasses and serve with wafer biscuits if liked.
Serves 6 to 8

LEFT: *Orange Ice Cream*
RIGHT: *Chocolate Mint Ice Cream; Ginger Snap Ice Cream*

CHOCOLATE MINT ICE CREAM

25 g (1 oz) custard powder
300 ml (½ pint) milk
1 × 170 g (6 oz) can evaporated milk
2 eggs, separated
40 g (1½ oz) icing sugar
25 g (1 oz) butter
½ teaspoon peppermint flavouring
½ teaspoon green food colouring

TOPPING:
50 g (2 oz) chocolate, melted and cooled
2 tablespoons single cream

TO DECORATE:
3-4 tablespoons double cream, whipped

Blend the custard powder with 2 tablespoons milk in a large bowl. Heat the remaining milk and evaporated milk until boiling and stir into the mixture. Return to the pan and heat, stirring, until very thick.

Return to the bowl and beat in the egg yolks, one at a time. Beat in the icing sugar, butter, flavouring and colouring and set aside until cold, whisking occasionally.

Whisk the egg whites until very stiff and fold into the cold custard. Transfer to a rigid freezerproof container, cover and freeze for about 1 hour, until beginning to freeze. Whisk well, re-cover and partially freeze again. Repeat process twice.

Spoon into individual freezerproof dishes. Cover and freeze until firm.

Combine the chocolate and cream and spoon over the ice cream. Decorate with piped cream.

Serves 4 to 6

GINGER SNAP ICE CREAM

3 eggs, separated
50 g (2 oz) soft dark brown sugar
4 tablespoons green ginger wine
50 g (2 oz) butter, melted
150 g (5 oz) ginger biscuits, finely crushed
284 ml (10 fl oz) double cream

Place the egg yolks in a mixing bowl over a pan of hot water. Add the sugar and half the ginger wine and whisk until pale and creamy. Remove from the heat and whisk until cool. Stir in 1 tablespoon of the remaining ginger wine, the melted butter and all but 25 g (1 oz) of the biscuit crumbs.

Whisk the cream and egg whites together until stiff enough to form soft peaks. Whisk in the remaining ginger wine. Fold both mixtures together and transfer to a rigid freezerproof container. Cover with clingfilm and freeze for about 1 hour, until just beginning to freeze around the edge. Whisk well, re-cover and partially freeze again. Repeat the process at least twice more. Cover, seal and freeze until firm.

Transfer to the refrigerator 30 minutes before serving. Scoop into chilled glasses and sprinkle with the remaining biscuit crumbs.

Serves 6 to 8

ICED STRAWBERRY RING

568 ml (1 pint)
  whipping cream
2 tablespoons brandy
1 tablespoon icing
  sugar, sifted
125 g (4 oz)
  meringues
TO FINISH:
142 ml (5 fl oz)
  double cream,
  whipped
350 g (12 oz)
  strawberries,
  halved

Place the cream, brandy and icing sugar in a bowl and whip until it stands in soft peaks. Break the meringues into pieces and fold into the cream.

Turn into a 1.5 litre (2½ pint) ring mould. Cover with foil, seal and freeze until firm.

Turn out onto a serving dish 30 minutes before serving and place in the refrigerator. Pipe cream around the edge and fill the centre with strawberries to serve.

Serves 8

BOMBE NOËL

50 g (2 oz) glacé
  cherries
50 g (2 oz) angelica
50 g (2 oz)
  crystallized
  pineapple
50 g (2 oz)
  crystallized ginger
50 g (2 oz) raisins
2 tablespoons brandy
2 tablespoons
  Cointreau
3 egg yolks
75 g (3 oz) caster
  sugar
284 ml (10 fl oz)
  single cream
few drops of vanilla
  essence
284 ml (10 fl oz)
  double cream,
  whipped
TO DECORATE:
angelica and
  crystallized
  pineapple

Chop the cherries, angelica, pineapple and ginger and place in a bowl. Add the raisins. Pour on the brandy and Cointreau. Leave to soak for 1 hour.

Beat the egg yolks and sugar together until creamy. Bring the single cream slowly to the boil, then pour onto the egg mixture, stirring vigorously. Strain, add the vanilla and leave to cool.

Fold half the cream and the fruit into the custard. Place in a rigid freezerproof container. Cover and freeze for 1 hour. Remove from the freezer and stir well. Turn into a 1.5 litre (2½ pint) freezerproof pudding basin, cover with foil and freeze until firm.

Dip the basin into cold water and turn the bombe out onto a chilled serving plate. Pipe the remaining cream in rosettes around the bombe and decorate with diamonds of angelica and pieces of pineapple.

Serves 6 to 8

STRAWBERRY ICE CREAM

350 g (12 oz)
  strawberries
15 g (½ oz) gelatine,
  soaked in 3
  tablespoons cold
  water
1 × 426 ml (¾ pint)
  can evaporated
  milk, chilled
175 g (6 oz) caster
  sugar
few drops of red food
  colouring
juice of ½ lemon
8 strawberries to
  decorate

Rub the strawberries through a sieve or purée in an electric blender and sieve to remove pips; there should be 300 ml (½ pint) purée.

Place the soaked gelatine in a bowl over a pan of simmering water and stir until dissolved. Add to the strawberry purée.

Whisk the evaporated milk until thick then add the sugar, strawberry purée, colouring and lemon juice. Turn into a rigid freezerproof container. Cover, seal and freeze for 1 hour.

Remove from the freezer and stir well, then re-freeze until solid. Transfer to the refrigerator 1 hour before serving to soften. Scoop into chilled glasses and decorate each with a strawberry.

Serves 8

PINEAPPLE ICE CREAM

1 large pineapple
3 egg whites
175 g (6 oz) caster
  sugar
284 ml (10 fl oz)
  double cream,
  whipped

Cut the pineapple in half lengthways. Scrape out the flesh and juice into a bowl, discarding the hard core. Chill the pineapple shells in the refrigerator; chop the flesh finely or purée in an electric blender or food processor.

Whisk the egg whites until stiff then gradually add the sugar, whisking continuously. Fold in the cream and chopped pineapple.

Place in a rigid freezerproof container. Cover, seal and freeze for 1 hour. Remove from the freezer, stir well, then re-freeze until solid.

Transfer the pineapple ice to the refrigerator 30 minutes before serving to soften. Scoop into the chilled pineapple shells and arrange on a serving dish. Scoop the ice cream into individual chilled glass dishes to serve.

Serves 6 to 8

Strawberry Ice Cream; Pineapple Ice Cream; Bombe Noël

GRAPEFRUIT SORBET

2 grapefruit
    (preferably pink)
1 envelope gelatine,
    dissolved in 2
    tablespoons water
600 ml (1 pint)
    grapefruit juice
25 g (1 oz) caster
    sugar
150 g (5.2 oz)
    natural yogurt
2 egg whites, stiffly
    beaten
8 mint sprigs to
    decorate

Finely grate the rind from both grapefruit. Place in a large bowl and add just enough boiling water to cover. Leave to soak for 5 minutes, then drain.

Cut the grapefruit in half and squeeze thoroughly so that the flesh comes out with the juice. Add to the soaked rind, together with the dissolved gelatine, grapefruit juice, sugar and yogurt. Stir well, then transfer to a rigid freezerproof container, cover with clingfilm and freeze for about 1 hour, until just beginning to freeze around the edge. Whisk, then fold in the egg whites. Partly freeze and whisk twice more. Cover, seal and freeze until firm.

Transfer to the refrigerator 10 minutes before serving to soften. Scoop into chilled glasses and decorate with mint sprigs.
Serves 8

PEAR SORBET

4 dessert pears
150 ml (¼ pint)
    water
75 g (3 oz) sugar
white wine (optional
    – see method)
1 egg white
2 tablespoons grated
    chocolate

Peel, quarter and core the pears. Place in a pan with the water and sugar and cook gently for about 10 minutes, until tender.

Place the pears and syrup in an electric blender or food processor and work to a purée. Make up to 600 ml (1 pint) with water or white wine. Pour into a rigid freezerproof container, cover, seal and freeze for 2 hours, until mushy.

Whisk the egg white until stiff, then whisk into the ice. Return to the freezer for 2 hours, then whisk again and freeze until firm.

Transfer to the refrigerator 30 to 50 minutes before serving, to soften. Scoop into chilled glasses and sprinkle with the chocolate to serve.
Serves 4

EARL GREY SORBET

A delicately flavoured sorbet which can be served as a dessert accompanied by biscuits (see pages 147 to 152), or as a 'refresher' between the starter and main course.

4 teaspoons Earl
    Grey tea
450 ml (¾ pint)
    boiling water
finely pared rind and
    juice of 1 lemon
75 g (3 oz) sugar
2 egg whites

Put the tea in a basin and pour over the boiling water. Add the lemon rind, juice and sugar. Leave until cold, then strain into a rigid freezerproof container. Cover, seal and freeze for about 2 hours, until mushy.

Whisk the egg whites until stiff, then whisk into the ice. Return to the freezer for 2 hours, then whisk again and freeze until firm.

Transfer to the refrigerator 30 to 50 minutes before serving, to soften. Scoop into chilled glasses to serve.
Serves 4

Grapefruit Sorbet

ELDERFLOWER SORBET

450 ml (¾ pint)
  water
125 g (4 oz) caster
  sugar
thinly pared rind and
  juice of 2 lemons
25 g (1 oz)
  elderflower heads
1 egg white
elderflower or mint
  leaves to decorate

Put the water, sugar and lemon rind in a pan and heat gently, stirring, until the sugar has dissolved. Bring to the boil, then simmer for 5 minutes. Add the elderflower and lemon juice, cover and leave to cool.

Strain into a rigid freezerproof container, cover, seal and freeze for 2 to 3 hours, until half frozen.

Whisk the egg white until stiff, then whisk into the ice. Cover, seal and freeze until firm.

Transfer to the refrigerator 10 minutes before serving to soften. Scoop into chilled glasses and top with elderflower or mint leaves.
Serves 6

THYME AND HONEY SORBET

4 large lemons
600 ml (1 pint) water
75 g (3 oz) caster
  sugar
large bunch of thyme
3 tablespoons clear
  honey
1 egg white
4 thyme sprigs to
  decorate

Cut a thin slice from the base of each lemon so that they will stand. Cut the tops off the lemons and carefully scrape out the flesh. Sieve to extract the juice. Reserve the shells.

Put the water, sugar and thyme in a pan and heat gently until the sugar has dissolved. Bring to the boil, then simmer for 3 minutes. Add the honey and lemon juice. Cool.

Strain into a rigid freezerproof container, cover, seal and freeze for 2 to 3 hours, until half frozen.

Whisk the egg white until stiff, then whisk into the ice. Spoon the sorbet into the lemon shells, piling it up well. Place upright on a tray and freeze for 2 hours, until solid. Freeze any remaining sorbet in a rigid container, for another occasion.

Transfer to the refrigerator 10 minutes before serving to soften. Decorate with thyme sprigs.
Serves 4

Elderflower Sorbet; Thyme and Honey Sorbet

BLACKBERRY ICE CREAM

500 g (1 lb)
  blackberries
2 tablespoons caster
  sugar
120 ml (4 fl oz)
  water
50 g (2 oz)
  granulated sugar
3 egg yolks
426 ml (15 fl oz)
  single cream
2 tablespoons icing
  sugar, sifted
2 tablespoons rose
  water
wafer biscuits to
  serve

Put the blackberries in a pan with the caster sugar and simmer gently for 10 minutes or until tender. Rub through a sieve and leave to cool.

Put the water and granulated sugar in a pan and heat gently, stirring, until dissolved. Increase the heat and boil steadily until the syrup reaches a temperature of 110°C (230°F). At this stage a little of the cooled syrup will form a thread when drawn between the thumb and forefinger.

Cool slightly then pour onto the egg yolks, whisking until the mixture is thick and mousse-like. Mix the cream with the fruit purée, icing sugar and rose water and fold into the mousse.

Turn into a rigid freezerproof container. Cover, seal and freeze.

Transfer to the refrigerator 1 hour before serving to soften. Scoop into chilled glasses and serve with wafer biscuits.
Serves 8

ICED MOCHA MOUSSES

3 eggs, separated
75 g (3 oz) caster
  sugar
50 g (2 oz) plain
  chocolate, chopped
1 tablespoon instant
  coffee powder
2 tablespoons water
142 ml (5 fl oz)
  double cream,
  whipped
grated chocolate to
  decorate

Whisk the egg yolks with the sugar until thick and creamy.

Place the chocolate, coffee and water in a bowl over a pan of hot water and heat gently until melted, then whisk into the egg mixture. Fold in the cream.

Whisk the egg whites until stiff and carefully fold into the mousse. Pour into individual freezerproof ramekin dishes. Cover, seal and freeze for 3 to 4 hours.

Transfer to the refrigerator 10 minutes before serving to soften. Decorate with grated chocolate.
Serves 4 to 6

FROZEN APRICOT MOUSSE

250 g (8 oz) dried
  apricots, soaked
  overnight in 450 ml
  (¾ pint) water
3 eggs, separated
75 g (3 oz) soft
  brown sugar
284 ml (10 fl oz)
  double cream,
  whipped

Put the apricots in a pan with their soaking water and simmer for 15 to 20 minutes, until softened. Drain, reserving the liquid; cool slightly.

Place the apricots in an electric blender or food processor and work to a purée, adding a little of the cooking liquid if necessary.

Whisk the egg yolks and sugar until pale, then fold in the apricot purée. Whisk the egg whites until stiff and fold into the mixture with the cream.

Pour into a 1.2 litre (2 pint) freezerproof bowl, cover, seal and freeze until firm.

Transfer to the refrigerator 30 to 50 minutes before serving to soften. Scoop into chilled dishes to serve.
Serves 6

LEFT: *Blackberry Ice Cream*
OPPOSITE: *Brown Bread Ice Cream*

PINEAPPLE SORBET

1 × 382 g (13½ oz) can crushed pineapple
50 g (2 oz) caster sugar
1 tablespoon lemon juice
300 g (10 oz) natural low-fat yogurt

Drain the pineapple and pour the juice into a pan. Add the sugar and lemon juice and heat until dissolved. Allow to cool thoroughly, then stir in the yogurt.

Pour into a shallow rigid container and freeze until the mixture is mushy. Remove from the freezer and stir in the crushed pineapple. Return to a rigid container, cover and freeze until solid.

Transfer to the refrigerator about 1 hour before required. Spoon into sundae dishes to serve.
Serves 6

CRUNCHY HAZELNUT ICE

75 g (3 oz) wholemeal breadcrumbs
50 g (2 oz) hazelnuts, ground
175 g (6 oz) muscovado sugar
3 egg whites
300 g (10 oz) natural low-fat yogurt

Mix together the breadcrumbs, hazelnuts and 50 g (2 oz) of the sugar. Spread on a baking sheet. Place under a preheated hot grill for about 2 minutes until golden brown, stirring occasionally. Leave to cool.

Whisk the egg whites until stiff, then gradually whisk in the remaining sugar. Fold in the yogurt and breadcrumb mixture. Turn into a rigid freezerproof container. Cover, seal and freeze until firm.

Transfer to the refrigerator 30 minutes before serving to soften. Scoop into chilled glasses to serve.
Serves 6 to 8

FREEZING ICES

If you have freezer space you can always double or treble the quantities of these ices and sorbets.

The most suitable containers for freezing ice creams are rigid polythene boxes with airtight lids. Although fairly expensive to buy, they are re-usable and will last for many years. Metal containers are also suitable. Because all liquids expand slightly on freezing, it is important to leave a space of about 2 cm (¾ inch) at the top of the container to prevent the lid being forced off.

BROWN BREAD ICE CREAM

75 g (3 oz) wholemeal breadcrumbs
50 g (2 oz) demerara sugar
50 g (2 oz) hazelnuts, skinned and ground
3 egg whites
125 g (4 oz) caster sugar
426 ml (15 fl oz) double cream, lightly whipped
18 hazelnuts, to decorate

Combine the breadcrumbs, demerara sugar and hazelnuts on a heatproof plate. Place under a preheated hot grill until golden brown, stirring occasionally. Leave to cool.

Whisk the egg whites until stiff, then gradually whisk in the caster sugar. Fold two-thirds of the cream into the meringue with the breadcrumb mixture.

Turn into a 1.2 litre (2 pint) freezerproof mould. Cover, seal and freeze until solid.

Turn out onto a plate 30 minutes before serving. Decorate with the remaining cream and the hazelnuts. Leave in the refrigerator to soften until required.
Serves 6 to 8

RASPBERRY SORBET

500 g (1 lb)
  raspberries
300 ml (½ pint)
  water
125 g (4 oz)
  granulated sugar
1 egg white

Work the raspberries in an electric blender or food processor until smooth, then work through a nylon sieve to remove the pips.

Heat the water and sugar gently in a pan, stirring, until the sugar has dissolved. Boil rapidly for 5 minutes, stir into the raspberry purée and leave to cool. Pour the mixture into a rigid freezerproof container, cover and freeze for 2 to 3 hours until half-frozen. Remove from the freezer and turn into a bowl. Whisk the egg white until stiff, then whisk into the half-frozen raspberry mixture.

Return the sorbet to the container, cover, seal and freeze.

Transfer to the refrigerator 10 minutes before serving to soften. Scoop into chilled glasses and serve immediately.
Serves 4 to 6

GOOSEBERRY ICE CREAM

500 g (1 lb)
  gooseberries
125 g (4 oz) caster
  sugar
2 tablespoons water
3 egg whites
75 g (3 oz) icing
  sugar, sifted
few drops of green
  food colouring
142 ml (5 fl oz)
  double cream,
  whipped

Place the gooseberries in a pan with the sugar and water. Cover and cook gently for 10 to 15 minutes until tender. Purée in an electric blender or food processor, then sieve. Leave to cool.

Whisk the egg whites until stiff, then gradually whisk in the icing sugar. Fold in the purée, food colouring and cream.

Turn into a rigid freezerproof container, cover, seal and freeze.

Transfer to the refrigerator 30 minutes before serving to soften. Scoop into chilled glasses to serve.
Serves 6 to 8

APRICOT SORBET

500 g (1 lb) fresh
  apricots, stoned
450 ml (¾ pint)
  water
juice of ½ lime or
  lemon
175 g (6 oz)
  granulated sugar
2 tablespoons kirsch
  or apricot brandy
1 egg white

Place the apricots in a pan with 150 ml (¼ pint) of the water. Cover and simmer gently for 15 minutes until tender. Cool slightly, then put the apricots in an electric blender or food processor with the lime or lemon juice and work until smooth.

Heat the remaining water and the sugar gently in a pan, stirring, until the sugar has dissolved. Boil rapidly for 5 minutes, then stir into the apricot purée and leave to cool completely.

Add the kirsch or brandy and pour the mixture into a rigid freezerproof container. Cover and freeze for 2 to 3 hours until half-frozen. Remove from the freezer and turn into a bowl. Whisk the egg white until stiff, then whisk into the half-frozen apricot mixture. Return the sorbet to the container, cover, seal and freeze.

Transfer to the refrigerator 10 minutes before serving to soften. Scoop into chilled glasses and serve immediately.
Serves 6 to 8

Raspberry Sorbet; Gooseberry Ice Cream; Apricot Sorbet

Raspberry Yogurt Sorbet

RASPBERRY YOGURT SORBET

250 g (8 oz)
  raspberries
2 × 150 g (5.2 oz)
  cartons natural
  yogurt
1 tablespoon gelatine,
  soaked in 3
  tablespoons cold
  water
2 egg whites
75 g (3 oz) caster
  sugar

Work the raspberries in an electric blender or food processor until smooth, then sieve to remove pips. Stir in the yogurt.

Heat the gelatine gently until dissolved then add to the purée.

Whisk the egg whites until stiff, then gradually whisk in the sugar. Carefully fold the purée into the meringue, turn into a rigid freezerproof container, cover, seal and freeze until firm.

Transfer to the refrigerator 30 minutes before serving to soften. Scoop into chilled glasses to serve.
Serves 6

MINT WATER ICE

450 ml (¾ pint)
  water
125 g (4 oz) sugar
thinly pared rind and
  juice of 2 lemons
25 g (1 oz) mint
  leaves
few drops of green
  food colouring
1 egg white
TO DECORATE:
small mint leaves
caster sugar for
  sprinkling

Put the water, sugar, lemon rind and juice in a pan and heat gently, stirring, until the sugar is dissolved. Bring to the boil and simmer for 5 minutes, then add the mint leaves, cover and leave to cool. Strain and add the colouring. Turn into a rigid freezerproof container. Cover, seal and freeze.

When half-frozen, whisk most of the egg white until stiff and fold into the water ice. Cover, seal and freeze until firm.

Brush the small mint leaves with the reserved egg white. Sprinkle with sugar and leave to dry for about 1 hour.

Transfer the water ice to the refrigerator 10 minutes before serving to soften. Scoop into chilled glasses and decorate with sugared mint leaves.
Serves 6

BLACKCURRANT WATER ICE

500 g (1 lb)
  blackcurrants
150 ml (¼ pint) +
  2 tablespoons water
125 g (4 oz) caster
  sugar
juice of ½ lemon
1 egg white, lightly
  whisked

Place the blackcurrants in a pan with 2 tablespoons of the water and simmer until tender. Rub through a sieve or purée in an electric blender or food processor; there should be 300 ml (½ pint) purée.

Place the sugar and remaining water in a pan and heat gently, stirring, until dissolved. Bring to the boil and simmer for 5 minutes; allow to cool. Add to the blackcurrant purée with the lemon juice. Turn into a rigid freezerproof container. Cover, seal and freeze.

When the water ice is half-frozen, fold in the egg white. Freeze until firm. Transfer to the refrigerator 10 minutes before serving to soften. Scoop into chilled glasses to serve.
Serves 4

BLACKCURRANT FREEZIES

*350 g (12 oz)
blackcurrants,
stalks removed
175 g (6 oz) caster
sugar
2 teaspoons gelatine,
soaked in 2
tablespoons water
426 ml (15 fl oz)
double cream,
whipped
2 egg whites
blackcurrant leaves to
decorate*

Place the blackcurrants in a pan with 75 g (3 oz) of the sugar. Cover and simmer gently for 15 minutes.

Cool slightly, then pour into an electric blender or food processor and work to a smooth purée. Turn into a bowl to cool.

Heat the gelatine gently until dissolved, then fold into the blackcurrant purée. Carefully fold in the whipped cream.

Whisk the egg whites until stiff, then gradually whisk in the remaining sugar. Fold into the blackcurrant mixture. Turn into 8 ramekins and freeze for 2 to 3 hours.

Decorate with blackcurrant leaves before serving.
Serves 8

REDCURRANT SHERBET

*500 g (1 lb)
redcurrants
125 g (4 oz) icing
sugar, sifted
juice of 1 orange
1 egg white*
TO DECORATE:
*frosted currant leaves
(see below)
few sprigs redcurrants*

Place the redcurrants, icing sugar and orange juice in an electric blender or food processor and work to a purée. Sieve to remove the pips. Place in a rigid freezerproof container, cover, seal and freeze for 2 to 3 hours. Whisk to break up the crystals.

Whisk the egg white until stiff, then whisk into the half-frozen purée. Return to the freezer until firm. Transfer to the refrigerator 15 minutes before serving to soften.

Scoop into chilled glasses and decorate with frosted currant leaves and redcurrant sprigs.
Serves 4

Frosted leaves: Paint egg white all over the leaves with a fine paintbrush. Brush off any excess and dip the leaves in caster sugar until completely coated. Place on greaseproof paper to dry for 1 to 2 hours.

Redcurrant Sherbet

STRAWBERRY ICE CREAM SOUFFLÉ

*500 g (1 lb)
strawberries
4 eggs, separated
175 g (6 oz) caster
sugar
284 ml (10 fl oz)
double cream,
whipped*

Tie a band of foil very tightly around a 900 ml (1½ pint) freezerproof soufflé dish to stand 5 cm (2 inches) above the rim.

Reserve 6 strawberries for decoration. Work the remainder in an electric blender or food processor to a purée. Sieve to remove pips.

Place the egg yolks and sugar in a bowl and whisk with an electric mixer until thick and creamy. Fold the purée into the cream, then fold into the egg mixture. Whisk the egg whites until stiff, then carefully fold into the strawberry mixture. Turn into the dish and freeze until firm.

Transfer to the refrigerator 30 minutes before serving to soften slightly. Remove the foil carefully.

Decorate the soufflé with strawberry slices before serving.
Serves 8

PINEAPPLE PARFAIT

1 large pineapple
125 g (4 oz) caster
  sugar
2 egg whites
284 ml (10 fl oz)
  double cream,
  whipped
2 tablespoons kirsch

Cut the pineapple in half lengthways.
Scrape out the flesh and juice into an
electric blender or food processor.
Add 1 tablespoon of the sugar and
work to a purée.

Transfer to a rigid freezerproof
container, cover, seal and freeze for
1 to 2 hours, until half frozen.

Whisk the egg whites until stiff,
then whisk in the remaining sugar, a
tablespoon at a time. Whisk the half
frozen purée, then fold into the
meringue mixture with the cream
and kirsch.

Spoon into chilled glasses and
serve immediately.
Serves 6 to 8

PINA COLADA ICE

1 large pineapple
25 g (1 oz) creamed
  coconut, chopped
2 tablespoons boiling
  water
2 egg whites
125 g (4 oz) caster
  sugar
6 tablespoons white
  rum
284 ml (10 fl oz)
  whipping cream,
  whipped

Cut the pineapple in half lengthways.
Scrape out the flesh and juice into a
bowl, discarding the hard core. Chill
the shells in the refrigerator. Work
the flesh and juice in an electric
blender or food processor to make a
purée.

Blend the coconut cream with the
boiling water; leave to cool.

Whisk the egg whites until stiff,
then gradually whisk in the sugar.

Mix the pineapple purée with the
coconut and rum. Fold this into the
cream with the meringue mixture.
Turn into a rigid freezerproof
container, cover, seal and freeze for
1½ hours. Remove from the freezer
and stir well, then re-freeze until
firm.

Transfer to the refrigerator
30 minutes before serving to soften.
Scoop into the chilled pineapple
shells and arrange on a dish.
Serves 8 to 10

Pineapple Parfait; Pina Colada Ice

GINGER ICE CREAM

120 ml (4 fl oz)
  water
75 g (3 oz)
  granulated sugar
3 egg yolks
284 ml (10 fl oz)
  double cream
75 g (3 oz) preserved
  stem ginger, finely
  chopped

Place the water and sugar in a pan and heat gently, stirring until dissolved. Increase the heat and boil steadily until the syrup reaches a temperature of 110°C (225°F); at this stage a little of the cooled syrup will form a thread when drawn between the thumb and forefinger.

Cool slightly, then pour onto the egg yolks, whisking until the mixture is thick and mousse-like.

Whip the cream until it stands in soft peaks, then fold in the ginger. Fold into the egg mixture. Turn into a rigid freezerproof container. Cover, seal and freeze until firm.

Transfer to the refrigerator 20 minutes before serving to soften. Scoop into chilled glasses to serve.
Serves 4 to 6

RUM AND RAISIN ICE

75 g (3 oz) seedless
  raisins
4 tablespoons dark
  rum
3 egg yolks
125 g (4 oz) soft
  brown sugar
284 ml (10 fl oz)
  single cream
284 ml (10 fl oz)
  double cream,
  whipped

Soak the raisins in the rum in a bowl.

Place the egg yolks and sugar in a heatproof bowl and whisk, using an electric mixer, until thick and mousse-like. Bring the single cream to just below boiling point and stir into the egg mixture. Place the bowl over a pan of simmering water and stir until thickened. Strain and cool.

Fold the double cream into the cooled custard mixture. Transfer to a rigid freezerproof container, cover, seal and freeze for 2 to 3 hours, until there is 2.5 cm (1 inch) of solid ice cream around the sides. Mix until smooth, then stir in the rum and raisins. Return to the freezer until firm.

Transfer to the refrigerator 20 minutes before serving to soften. Scoop into chilled glasses to serve.
Serves 8

Ginger Ice Cream; Rum and Raisin Ice; Maple and Walnut Ice

MAPLE AND WALNUT ICE

426 ml (15 fl oz)
  double cream
142 ml (5 fl oz)
  single cream
25 g (1 oz) soft
  brown sugar
6 tablespoons maple
  syrup
4 tablespoons dark
  rum
75 g (3 oz) walnut
  pieces, chopped

Place the creams, sugar, syrup and rum in a bowl and whip until it holds its shape. Fold in the nuts. Turn into a rigid freezerproof container, cover, seal and freeze until firm.

Transfer to the refrigerator 30 minutes before serving to soften. Scoop into chilled glass dishes. Serve with Fudge Sauce (see page 153), or extra maple syrup, and Langue de Chat biscuits (see page 149).
Serves 6

APPLE AND BLACKCURRANT ICE CREAM

250 g (8 oz) cooking
apples, peeled,
cored and sliced
250 g (8 oz)
blackcurrants
2 tablespoons
granulated sugar
4 tablespoons water
4 eggs, separated
125 g (4 oz) caster
sugar
284 ml (10 fl oz)
double cream,
whipped
frosted currant leaves
(see Redcurrant
Sherbet, page 43)
to decorate

Place the apples in a large pan with the blackcurrants, granulated sugar and water. Cover and cook over a gentle heat until soft.

Cool slightly, then work in an electric blender or food processor to make a purée. Sieve to remove pips and leave to cool completely.

Whisk the egg whites until stiff, then gradually whisk in the caster sugar; whisk in the egg yolks. Fold the fruit purée into the cream, then fold into the egg mixture. Turn into a rigid freezerproof container, cover, seal and freeze until firm.

Transfer to the refrigerator 30 minutes before serving to soften.

Scoop into chilled glasses and decorate with frosted currant leaves.
Serves 8 to 10

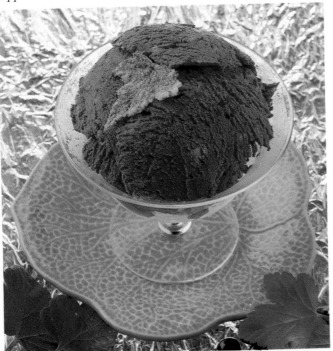

Apple and Blackcurrant Ice Cream

COFFEE GRANITA

75 g (3 oz) soft
brown sugar
600 ml (1 pint)
water
2 tablespoons coffee
granules
TOPPING:
2 tablespoons Tia
Maria
120 ml (4 fl oz)
whipping cream,
whipped
1 teaspoon coffee
granules

Place the sugar and water in a heavy-based pan and heat gently until dissolved. Bring to the boil; boil for 5 minutes, add the coffee; cool.

Pour into a rigid freezerproof container, cover, seal and freeze for 2 hours. Whisk and return to the freezer for 2 hours. Whisk again and return to the freezer until firm.

Leave at room temperature for 10 minutes, then stir until crumbly. Spoon into tall glasses. Pour a little liqueur over each, top with a whirl of cream, and sprinkle with coffee.
Serves 4 to 6

LEMON GRANITA

125 g (4 oz) caster
sugar
600 ml (1 pint)
water
thinly pared rind and
juice of 3 lemons
4 lemon twists to
decorate

Gently heat the sugar and water in a pan with the lemon rind until dissolved, then boil for 5 minutes. Add the lemon juice, cool, then strain.

Freeze and serve as for Coffee Granita (above), replacing the topping with lemon twists.
Serves 4

GOOSEBERRY SORBET

500 g (1 lb)
gooseberries
2 heads elderflower,
tied in muslin
(optional)
125 g (4 oz) sugar
150 ml (¼ pint)
water
1 egg white
mint leaves to
decorate

Put the gooseberries in a pan with the elderflower, if using, sugar and water. Cover and simmer for 15 minutes until tender. Remove the elderflower, cool slightly, then work in an electric blender or food processor until smooth. Sieve, then leave to cool.

Turn into a rigid freezerproof container, cover, seal and freeze for 2 to 3 hours, until slushy.

Whisk the egg white until stiff and fold into the purée. Freeze until firm.

Transfer to refrigerator 10 minutes before serving to soften. Scoop into glasses and decorate with mint leaves.
Serves 4

MELON SHERBET

1 melon (preferably
 Charentais),
 weighing 1 kg
 (2 lb)
50 g (2 oz) icing
 sugar
juice of 1 lime or
 small lemon
1 egg white

Cut the melon in half, scoop out and discard the seeds. Scoop out the flesh with a spoon and reserve the shells. Place the flesh in an electric blender or food processor with the icing sugar and lime or lemon juice. Work to a purée, then pour into a rigid freezerproof container, cover, seal and freeze for 2 to 3 hours.

Whisk to break up the ice crystals. Whisk the egg white until stiff, then whisk into the half-frozen melon mixture. Return to the freezer until firm.

Transfer to the refrigerator 20 minutes before serving to soften. Scoop into the melon shells.
Serves 4 to 6

WATERMELON ICE

½ small watermelon,
 weighing about
 1.25 kg (2½ lb)
125 g (4 oz) icing
 sugar, sifted
juice of 1 small lemon
mint sprigs to
 decorate

Discard the seeds and scoop out the flesh from the watermelon, reserving the shell. Cut the shell into 4 wedges. Place in a freezerproof bowl of matching size and re-shape. Chill.

Place the flesh in a blender or food processor with the sugar and lemon juice and work until smooth. Pour into a rigid freezerproof container and freeze for 3 to 4 hours. Turn into a chilled bowl and whisk until fluffy.

Turn into the melon shell and smooth the top. Cover with foil and freeze until solid.

Separate the melon wedges, using a warmed knife, 10 minutes before serving. Decorate with mint sprigs.
Serves 4

Coffee Granita; Lemon Granita; Gooseberry Sorbet

SOUFFLÉS, MOUSSES AND LIGHT DESSERTS

Soufflés are probably the most impressive of all desserts – guaranteed to be complimented by your guests. Both hot and cold soufflés should stand proud of their characteristic straight-sided dish when served. Hot soufflés rise during cooking and must be served immediately, as they quickly lose that wonderful puffy appearance. By contrast cold soufflés, which are set with gelatine, can be prepared well in advance. A cold soufflé is prepared so that when served it appears to have risen above the edge of the dish (see page 51). It can be decorated with chopped toasted nuts or crushed ratafias to give a sophisticated finish.

Like soufflés, mousses are light, creamy desserts which depend on the versatile egg for their airy texture. They can be based on fruit purées or custard sauces. Fruit mousses, such as Bramble Mousse (page 69) and Gooseberry Mousse (page 68) are particularly delicious. Make them with fresh fruit in season or with fruit purées from the freezer at other times of the year.

Contrary to popular belief, soufflés and mousses are not difficult to make. Their success largely depends on whisking the egg whites adequately and folding them into the mixture carefully. When preparation time is short, choose from the other light desserts in this chapter: tangy fruit fools, fluffy soufflé omelets, simple fruit whips and delicious crèmes. Serve them with crisp biscuits and wafers for a perfect contrast in texture.

CHOCOLATE CINNAMON SOUFFLÉ

1 tablespoon cocoa powder
2 tablespoons boiling water
4 eggs, separated
125 g (4 oz) caster sugar
1½ teaspoons ground cinnamon
1 envelope gelatine, dissolved in 2 tablespoons water (see page 60)
142 ml (5 fl oz) whipping cream, half whipped
TO DECORATE:
150 g (6 oz) plain chocolate

Blend the cocoa with the boiling water to a smooth paste; cool.

Put the egg yolks, sugar, cinnamon and cocoa paste in a mixing bowl over a pan of simmering water. Whisk until creamy and thick enough to leave a trail. Remove from the heat and whisk until cool. Whisk the egg whites until stiff.

Pour the dissolved gelatine into the chocolate mixture in a slow continuous stream, stirring gently. Carefully fold in the half-whipped cream and whisked egg whites.

Turn into a prepared 900 ml (1½ pint) cold soufflé dish and chill for 2 hours or until set. Meanwhile, shave half the chocolate into curls, using a potato peeler; finely grate the remainder.

Carefully peel off the paper band from the soufflé and press the grated chocolate around the sides. Arrange the chocolate curls on top.
Serves 4 to 6

CRYSTALLIZED GINGER SOUFFLÉ

50-75 g (2-3 oz) crystallized ginger, minced or finely chopped
2 tablespoons boiling water
4 eggs, separated
25 g (1 oz) caster sugar
1 envelope gelatine, dissolved in 2 tablespoons water (see page 60)
142 ml (5 fl oz) whipping cream, half whipped
TO DECORATE:
50-75 g (2-3 oz) chopped nuts
few pieces crystallized ginger, chopped

Put the ginger in a mixing bowl and sprinkle on the boiling water. Add the egg yolks and sugar and place the bowl over a pan of simmering water. Whisk until creamy and thick enough to leave a trail. Remove from pan and whisk until cool. Whisk the egg whites until stiff.

Pour the dissolved gelatine into the ginger mixture in a slow continuous stream, stirring gently.

Carefully fold in the half-whipped cream, reserving 2 tablespoons for decoration, and the whisked egg whites. Turn into a prepared 900 ml (1½ pint) cold soufflé dish and chill for 2 hours or until set.

Peel off the paper band and press the nuts around the side. Decorate with the reserved cream and ginger.
Serves 4 to 6

Pineapple Soufflé: Replace the ginger with 75-125 g (3-4 oz) crystallized pineapple.

GOOSEBERRY SOUFFLÉ

500 g (1 lb)
    gooseberries
150 ml (¼ pint)
    water
125 g (4 oz) sugar
2 heads elderflower,
    tied in muslin
    (optional)
4 eggs, separated
75 g (3 oz) caster
    sugar
15 g (½ oz) gelatine,
    soaked in
    3 tablespoons cold
    water
few drops of green
    food colouring
142 ml (5 fl oz)
    whipping cream,
    whipped
TO DECORATE:
2 tablespoons
    chopped almonds,
    toasted
4 tablespoons double
    cream, whipped

Tie a band of double greaseproof paper around a 15 cm (6 inch) soufflé dish to stand 5 cm (2 inches) above the rim; oil the inside of the paper.

Place the gooseberries in a pan with the water, sugar and elderflower, if using. Cover and simmer gently for 10 to 15 minutes, until tender. Remove the elderflower, rub through a sieve or work in an electric blender until smooth. Leave to cool.

Place the egg yolks and sugar in a bowl and whisk over a pan of gently simmering water until thick.

Place the soaked gelatine in a bowl over a pan of simmering water and stir until dissolved. Add to the gooseberry purée, then carefully fold into the mousse, with the food colouring. Fold in the cream.

Whisk the egg whites until stiff; fold into the mousse when it is beginning to set. Turn into the prepared soufflé dish and leave to set in the refrigerator.

Remove the paper carefully and press the nuts around the sides. Decorate with piped cream rosettes.
Serves 6

LEMON SOUFFLÉ

3 large eggs,
    separated
175 g (6 oz) caster
    sugar
grated rind and juice
    of 2 lemons
426 ml (15 fl oz)
    whipping cream,
    whipped
15 g (½ oz)
    gelatine, soaked in
    3 tablespoons cold
    water
2 tablespoons
    chopped almonds,
    toasted, to decorate

Tie a band of double greaseproof paper around a 15 cm (6 inch) soufflé dish to stand 5 cm (2 inches) above the rim; oil the inside of the paper.

Place the egg yolks, sugar and lemon rind in a bowl. Heat the lemon juice in a small pan, then pour over the egg mixture. Whisk, using an electric beater, until thick, then fold in two-thirds of the cream.

Stir the soaked gelatine in a bowl over a pan of simmering water until dissolved. Add to the soufflé and stir carefully until beginning to set.

Whisk the egg whites until stiff, then fold into the mixture. Pour into the prepared dish and chill until set.

Remove the paper carefully and press the nuts around the sides. Spread some of the remaining cream over the top and pipe cream around the edge. Chill before serving.
Serves 6 to 8

┌─────────────────────────────────────┐
│ PREPARING SOUFFLÉ DISHES │
└─────────────────────────────────────┘

Traditionally a cold soufflé stands proud of its straight-sided dish and the top and sides are decorated – making this one of the most attractive desserts to serve.

The soufflé should stand at least 2.5 cm (1 inch) above the top of the dish. Cut a band of double greaseproof paper long enough to go around the outside of the dish and wide enough to stand about 5 cm (2 inches) above the rim. Secure with string or an elastic band and hold the paper together at the top with paper clips if necessary.

When the soufflé has set, remove the string or elastic band and paper clips, if used. Hold a palette knife against the side of the soufflé and carefully peel off the paper while sliding the knife around the soufflé.

OPPOSITE: *Chocolate Cinnamon Soufflé; Crystallized Ginger Soufflé*
RIGHT: *Lemon Soufflé*

SOUFFLÉ ROTHSCHILD

1 peach or mango,
   diced
1 kiwi fruit, sliced
8 strawberries, diced
2 slices fresh or
   canned pineapple,
   diced
1 miniature bottle
   Curaçao
4 eggs, separated
50 g (2 oz) caster
   sugar
25 g (1 oz) icing
   sugar, sifted, to
   serve

Place all the fruits in a shallow dish and pour over the Curaçao. Set aside for about 1 hour, turning the fruit occasionally.

Drain the excess juice from the fruit into a mixing bowl and add the egg yolks and caster sugar. Place over a pan of simmering water and whisk until creamy and thick enough to leave a trail. Remove from the pan and whisk until cool. Whisk the egg whites until stiff and carefully fold both mixtures together.

Place the fruit in a buttered 1.2 litre (2 pint) soufflé dish on a baking sheet. Spoon the soufflé mixture on top of the fruit.

Bake immediately in a preheated moderate oven, 180°C (350°F), Gas Mark 4, for 20 minutes. The soufflé should be well risen, golden brown on top and creamy in the centre.

Dredge with icing sugar and serve immediately.
Serves 4 to 6

Soufflé Rothschild

MILANAISE SOUFFLÉ

3 eggs, separated
75 g (3 oz) caster
   sugar
grated rind and juice
   of 2 lemons
1 envelope gelatine,
   dissolved in
   2 tablespoons
   water
142 ml (5 fl oz)
   whipping cream,
   half whipped
TO DECORATE:
50-75 g (2-3 oz)
   chopped nuts
crystallized lemon
   slices (optional)

Place the egg yolks, sugar, lemon rind and juice in a bowl over a pan of simmering water and whisk until thick enough to leave a trail. Remove from the pan and whisk until cool. Whisk egg whites until stiff.

Pour the dissolved gelatine into the lemon mixture in a slow continuous stream, stirring gently. Carefully fold in the cream, reserving 2 tablespoons for decoration, and the whisked egg whites. Turn into a prepared 900 ml (1½ pint) cold soufflé dish and chill for 2 hours or until set.

Peel off the paper and press nuts around side. Decorate with reserved cream and lemon slices, if wished.
Serves 4 to 6

Lime or Orange Soufflé: Replace the lemons with the grated rind and juice of 3 limes, or 2 oranges.
Coffee Soufflé: Replace the lemons with 2 tablespoons coffee granules dissolved in 2 tablespoons hot water.

TIPSY LEMON SOUFFLÉ

25 g (1 oz) sugar
3 tablespoons plain
   flour
175 ml (6 fl oz) milk
4 egg yolks, lightly
   beaten
50 g (2 oz) unsalted
   butter
4 tablespoons
   Cointreau
1 teaspoon grated
   lemon rind
1 tablespoon lemon
   juice
5 egg whites
pinch of salt

Place the sugar and flour in a pan and blend with a little of the milk. Stir in the remaining milk and heat, stirring, until the sauce thickens. Cook for 1 minute, then cool slightly and gradually beat in the egg yolks and butter. Heat, stirring, until the mixture becomes thick and smooth. Transfer to a large bowl and blend in the liqueur, lemon rind and juice.

Whisk the egg whites with the salt until stiff and fold into the lemon mixture, using a metal spoon. Turn into an oiled 20 cm (8 inch) soufflé dish; bake in a preheated moderately hot oven, 190°C (375°F), Gas Mark 5, for 45 minutes or until well risen and firm. Serve immediately.
Serves 6

BAKED CHOCOLATE SOUFFLÉ

25 g (1 oz) cocoa
    powder
40 g (1½ oz)
    cornflour
300 ml (½ pint)
    milk
50 g (2 oz) caster
    sugar
50 g (2 oz) butter
4 eggs, separated
1 teaspoon vanilla
    essence
25 g (1 oz) icing
    sugar, sifted, to
    serve

Blend the cocoa and cornflour with a little of the milk in a pan. Add the remaining milk, the sugar and butter and cook, stirring, until thickened. Cool slightly, then beat in the egg yolks, one at a time, and vanilla.

Whisk the egg whites until stiff. Fold about 2 tablespoons into the chocolate mixture, making it soft, then carefully fold in the remainder.

Turn into an oiled 1.2 litre (2 pint) soufflé dish and bake immediately in a preheated moderate oven, 180°C (350°F), Gas Mark 4, for 35 to 40 minutes, until risen and firm on top.

Sprinkle with icing sugar and serve immediately.
Serves 4

ALMOND SOUFFLÉ

50 g (2 oz) butter
50 g (2 oz) plain
    flour
4 tablespoons milk
5 eggs, separated
1 tablespoon sugar
4 tablespoons
    Amaretto or kirsch
    liqueur
4 macaroons (see
    page 150)
few flaked almonds to
    decorate

Prepare a 15 cm (6 inch) soufflé dish (see page 51).

Melt the butter in a saucepan and add the flour. Cook for 1 minute, then blend in the milk and cook, stirring, for a further 1 minute. Cool slightly. Beat the egg yolks thoroughly, then add to the sauce with the sugar and half the liqueur and beat well. Soak the macaroons in the remaining liqueur and set aside.

Whisk the egg whites until stiff, then fold lightly into the sauce. Arrange the soaked macaroons in the soufflé dish and pour the mixture over the top. Sprinkle with the almonds and place in a preheated moderately hot oven, 190°C (375°F), Gas Mark 5, for 30 minutes until well risen. Remove the collar and serve immediately.
Serves 4 to 6

Baked Chocolate Soufflé; Milanaise Soufflé

Soufflé Surprise

SOUFFLÉ SURPRISE

3 eggs, separated
50 g (2 oz) caster
  sugar
1 tablespoon sweet
  sherry
2 × 227 g (8 oz)
  packets frozen
  blackberries, half
  thawed
⅓ litre (12 oz) block
  vanilla ice cream
15 g (½ oz) icing
  sugar, sifted

Lightly butter a 1.5 litre (2½ pint) soufflé dish and place in a shallow dish or pan surrounded by ice cubes. Place in the refrigerator while preparing the soufflé mixture.

Put the egg yolks, sugar and sherry in a mixing bowl over a pan of simmering water and whisk until creamy and thick enough to leave a trail. Remove from the pan and whisk until cool.

Whisk the egg whites until stiff and, using a metal spoon, fold in the yolk mixture. Remove the prepared dish from the refrigerator and immediately put the blackberries in the bottom. Place the ice cream on top and quickly cover with the soufflé mixture.

Sprinkle with the icing sugar and bake immediately on the top shelf of a preheated moderately hot oven, 200°C (400°F), Gas Mark 6, for 8 to 10 minutes, until well risen and golden brown. Serve immediately.
Serves 4 to 6

SOUFFLÉ OMELET

2 eggs, separated
2 teaspoons cold
  water
2 teaspoons caster
  sugar
¼ teaspoon vanilla
  essence
15 g (½ oz) butter
2 tablespoons
  strawberry
  conserve
icing sugar for
  sprinkling

Whisk together the egg yolks, water, sugar and vanilla essence until pale and creamy. Whisk the egg whites until just stiff enough to stand in peaks, then gently fold both mixtures together with a metal spoon.

Melt the butter in a preheated pan until just beginning to sizzle. Add the egg mixture and spread evenly. Cook gently for about 2 minutes until set around the edge, then place under a preheated moderately hot grill for 1 to 2 minutes until the surface feels firm to the touch and looks puffy.

Heat the jam in a small pan. Put 2 skewers in a flame until red hot.

Remove the omelet from the oven and quickly spread with jam. Fold over with a palette knife and dredge thickly with icing sugar. Slide onto a hot dish and mark a lattice pattern across the top with the red hot skewers. Serve immediately.
Serves 1

Soufflé Omelet

APPLE OMELETS

4 eggs, separated
25 g (1 oz) caster
  sugar
2 teaspoons cornflour
½ teaspoon vanilla
  essence
25 g (1 oz) unsalted
  butter
FILLING:
50 g (2 oz) butter
2 tablespoons apricot
  jam
2 cooking apples,
  peeled, cored and
  sliced
25 g (1 oz) caster
  sugar
TO FINISH:
caster sugar for
  sprinkling

First make the filling: place the butter and apricot jam in a saucepan and heat until the butter is melted. Add the apples, cover and heat gently until just soft, then add the sugar.

To make the omelets, whisk together the egg yolks, sugar, cornflour and vanilla essence until thick and creamy. Whisk the egg whites until stiff and fold into the mixture.

Melt half the butter in a 23 cm (9 inch) frying pan. When just sizzling, pour in half the egg mixture. Cook slowly, without stirring, until just beginning to set and the underneath is golden.

Make a slit across the centre of the omelet, spoon half of the apple mixture onto one side of the omelet and fold over. Sprinkle with sugar. Cut in half and slide onto a warmed serving plate. Keep warm while making another omelet with the remaining ingredients. Serve immediately, with cream if desired.
Serves 2 to 4

SOUFFLÉ OMELETS

Soufflé omelets are usually filled with a sweet mixture and served as a dessert. For variety, make the soufflé omelet according to the instructions provided opposite, substituting one of the following fillings for the strawberry conserve. Quantities given are for one omelet.

ITALIAN-STYLE FILLING

2 scoops Neapolitan
  ice cream
2 teaspoons crunch-
  nut topping

Slide the unfolded omelet onto a serving plate, top with the ice cream, sprinkle with the nuts and serve immediately.

Soufflé Omelets with Swiss, French and Italian-style fillings

SWISS-STYLE FILLING

50 g (2 oz) plain
  chocolate
2 tablespoons black
  cherry conserve,
  warmed
icing sugar for
  sprinkling

Grate the chocolate coarsely or make curls with a potato peeler. Slide the unfolded omelet onto a warmed serving plate. Spread with the conserve and fold in half. Top with the chocolate and sprinkle lightly with icing sugar. Serve immediately.

FRENCH-STYLE FILLING

2 tablespoons orange
  marmalade,
  warmed
2 tablespoons
  Cointreau or
  Grand Marnier
grated rind of
  1 orange

While the omelet is still in the pan, spread with a little of the marmalade. Fold in half and turn onto a warmed serving plate. Stir the liqueur into the remaining marmalade, warm gently and pour over the omelet. Sprinkle with the orange rind and serve immediately.

COFFEE AND BRANDY SOUFFLÉ

3 eggs, separated
75 g (3 oz) caster
 sugar
300 ml (½ pint)
 milk
2 tablespoons instant
 coffee granules
15 g (½ oz) gelatine,
 soaked in
 3 tablespoons
 cold water
284 ml (10 fl oz)
 double cream
3 tablespoons brandy
2 tablespoons finely
 chopped almonds,
 browned

Prepare a 1 litre (1¾ pint) soufflé dish (see page 51).

Place the egg yolks and sugar in a bowl and beat until creamy. Place the milk in a pan with the coffee and bring to the boil. Pour onto the egg yolk mixture, stirring well. Return to the pan and cook gently, stirring constantly, until the custard coats the back of a spoon. Remove from the heat, add the gelatine and stir until dissolved. Leave to cool, stirring occasionally.

Place the cream in a bowl with the brandy and whip until stiff. Reserve a quarter for decoration.

When the custard is beginning to set, fold into the cream. Whisk the egg whites until stiff and stir 2 table-spoons into the coffee mixture to soften it. Carefully fold in remaining egg white and turn into the prepared dish. Leave to set in the refrigerator.

Remove the paper carefully and press the almonds around the side. Decorate with piped cream.
Serves 6 to 8

COFFEE AND WALNUT CREAM

12 marshmallows
120 ml (4 fl oz)
 strong black coffee
284 ml (10 fl oz)
 double cream
50 g (2 oz) walnut
 pieces, chopped

Place the marshmallows and coffee in a pan and heat gently, stirring until dissolved. Allow to cool.

Whip the cream until it stands in soft peaks, then carefully fold into the coffee mixture with all but 2 teaspoons of the walnuts.

Spoon into individual dishes and sprinkle with the remaining walnuts. Serve chilled.
Serves 4

Coffee and Brandy Soufflé; Coffee and Walnut Cream

AVOCADO AND LIME WHIP

2 ripe avocado pears,
  peeled and stoned
2 limes
6 tablespoons single
  cream
2 egg whites
50 g (2 oz) icing
  sugar, sifted

Chop the avocados and place in an electric blender or food processor. Strain the juice of 1 lime and add to the blender or processor with the cream. Work to a purée.

Whisk the egg whites until stiff, then whisk in the icing sugar, a tablespoon at a time. Carefully fold in the avocado mixture and spoon into individual glasses.

Slice half the remaining lime thinly, place a slice on each glass and spoon a little juice from the other half over each one. Serve immediately.
Serves 4

PASSION FRUIT WHIP

3 passion fruit
2 bananas
1 tablespoon lemon
  juice
142 ml (5 fl oz)
  double cream,
  whipped

Cut the passion fruit in half and scoop out the pulp. Mash bananas to a purée with the lemon juice, then mix with the passion fruit. Fold in the cream and spoon into individual serving dishes. Serve immediately.
Serves 4

MANGO MOUSSE

2 mangoes
75 g (3 oz) icing
  sugar, sifted
juice of 1 lime or
  small lemon
2 teaspoons gelatine,
  soaked in 2 table-
  spoons cold water
284 ml (10 fl oz)
  double cream,
  whipped
lime or lemon twists to
  decorate

Cut the mangoes in half lengthways, scrape out the flesh and place in a blender or food processor. Add the icing sugar and lime or lemon juice and blend until smooth.

Heat the gelatine gently until dissolved. Cool slightly, then mix into the mango purée with the cream. Pour into individual glass bowls and leave to set.

Decorate with lime or lemon twists.
Serves 6

Avocado and Lime Whip; Passion Fruit Whip; Mango Mousse

STRAWBERRY MOUSSE

350 g (12 oz)
    strawberries
2 eggs
1 egg yolk
75 g (3 oz) caster
    sugar
3 tablespoons orange
    juice
15 g (½ oz) gelatine
284 ml (10 fl oz)
    double cream,
    lightly whipped

Set aside a few strawberries for decoration. Sieve the remainder or purée in an electric blender, then sieve to remove pips; there should be 250 ml (8 fl oz) purée.

Place the eggs, egg yolk and sugar in a bowl and whisk over a pan of gently simmering water until thick.

Place the orange juice in a small pan, sprinkle over the gelatine and leave for 5 minutes. Heat gently to dissolve the gelatine, then fold into the egg mousse with the strawberry purée and half the cream.

Stir over a bowl of iced water until beginning to set, then turn into a 900 ml (1½ pint) ring mould. Chill until set.

Turn out onto a serving plate. Whip the remaining cream until stiff enough to pipe. Decorate the mousse with piped cream and the reserved strawberries.
Serves 8

GOOSEBERRY FOOL

500 g (1 lb)
    gooseberries
150 g (5 oz) caster
    sugar
2 heads of
    elderflower, tied in
    muslin (optional)
250 ml (8 fl oz)
    whipping cream,
    whipped
few drops of green
    food colouring
Langue de Chat
    biscuits (see page
    149) to serve

Place the gooseberries in a pan with the sugar and the elderflower, if using. Cover and cook for 10 to 15 minutes until tender. Remove the elderflower, and leave to cool. Rub through a sieve or work in an electric blender until smooth.

Fold the cream and colouring into the fruit mixture. Spoon into individual dishes and chill before serving, with Langue de Chat biscuits.
Serves 6

BANANA WHIP

4 bananas
1 egg white
25 g (1 oz) caster
    sugar
142 ml (5 fl oz)
    double cream,
    whipped
Cigarettes Russes
    (see page 149) to
    serve

Mash the bananas to a smooth purée. Whisk the egg white until stiff, then whisk in the sugar.

Fold the banana purée and meringue into the cream. Spoon into individual dishes and serve immediately, with Cigarettes Russes.
Serves 4 to 6

CALEDONIAN CREAM

2 tablespoons ginger
    marmalade
250 ml (8 fl oz)
    double cream
2 tablespoons caster
    sugar
2 tablespoons whisky
2 tablespoons lemon
    juice
2 egg whites
stem ginger slices

Divide the marmalade between 4 individual glass dishes.

Whip the cream until stiff, then fold in the caster sugar, whisky and lemon juice. Whisk the egg whites until stiff and fold into the cream mixture.

Spoon the cream mixture over the marmalade and decorate with the ginger.
Serves 4

LEFT: *Strawberry Mousse*
OPPOSITE: *Apple Tansy; Strawberry Fool; Raspberry Cream*

APPLE TANSY

*500 g (1 lb) cooking
apples, peeled,
cored and sliced
1 tablespoon water
25 g (1 oz) butter
2 eggs, separated
grated rind and juice
of 1 lemon
75 g (3 oz) caster
sugar
142 ml (5 fl oz)
double cream,
whipped
lemon slices to
decorate*

Place the apples in a pan with the
water and butter. Cover and simmer
until the apples are soft. Stir in the
egg yolks. Transfer to an electric
blender or food processor, add the
lemon rind and juice and work until
smooth.

Whisk the egg whites until stiff,
then gradually whisk in the sugar.
Fold in the apple mixture and the
cream and spoon into glasses. Chill
until required. Decorate with lemon
slices and serve with crisp biscuits.
Serves 4 to 6

STRAWBERRY FOOL

*350 g (12 oz)
strawberries
50 g (2 oz) caster
sugar
284 ml (10 fl oz)
double cream,
lightly whipped*

Set aside 3 strawberries for
decoration. Place the rest in an
electric blender or food processor
with the sugar and work until
smooth. Sieve to remove pips.

Fold the cream into the strawberry
purée. Spoon into glasses and chill.
Decorate with strawberry halves.
Serves 6

RASPBERRY CREAM

*500 g (1 lb)
raspberries
150 ml (¼ pint)
water
125 g (4 oz) sugar
15 g (½ oz) gelatine,
soaked in
3 tablespoons
cold water
284 ml (10 fl oz)
double cream,
lightly whipped*

Set aside 5 raspberries for decoration.
Place the rest in an electric blender or
food processor with the water and
sugar and work until smooth. Sieve
to remove pips.
Heat the gelatine gently until
dissolved, then stir into the raspberry
purée. When just beginning to set,
fold in three quarters of the cream.
Turn into an oiled 1.2 litre (2 pint)
mould and chill until set.

Whip remaining cream until thick.
Turn out the raspberry cream and
decorate with cream and raspberries.
Serves 6

ORANGE MOUSSE

4 eggs
2 egg yolks
125 g (4 oz) caster
    sugar
grated rind and juice
    of 1 lemon
15 g (½ oz) gelatine
284 ml (10 fl oz)
    whipping cream,
    whipped
184 g (6½ oz) can
    frozen concentrated
    orange juice,
    thawed
finely shredded
    orange rind to
    decorate

Place the eggs, egg yolks, sugar and lemon rind in a bowl and whisk over a pan of hot water until thick and mousse-like. Soak the gelatine in the lemon juice, adding water to make the juice up to 3 tablespoons if necessary.

Place the gelatine and lemon juice in a bowl over a pan of simmering water and stir until dissolved. Fold into the mousse with half the cream and the orange juice.

Stir gently over a bowl of iced water until beginning to set. Pour into a serving bowl and chill until set.

Decorate with piped cream and the orange rind.

Serves 6 to 8

APRICOT CREAM LAYER

250 g (8 oz) dried
    apricots, chopped
300 ml (½ pint)
    apple juice
142 ml (5 fl oz)
    double cream
1 tablespoon brandy
2 teaspoons icing
    sugar
1 tablespoon chopped
    almonds, toasted

Place the apricots in a pan with the apple juice and soak for 3 hours. Add 4 tablespoons water, bring to the boil and simmer gently for 30 minutes, until the apricots are soft. Cool.

Whip the cream with the brandy and icing sugar until it stands in soft peaks. Spoon half the apricot mixture into 4 glasses and cover with half the cream; repeat the layers. Sprinkle with the almonds and serve chilled.

Serves 4

USING GELATINE

Gelatine is used to set soufflés, mousses, jellies and other cold desserts. It must be used carefully to ensure good results.

To dissolve gelatine: place in a small bowl, add the cold water and leave for a few minutes until it swells and forms a stiff paste. Stand the bowl over a pan of hot water and stir until the gelatine dissolves to a completely clear liquid. Any cloudiness means it has not completely dissolved and will not set the mixture. Never boil the gelatine – it will become stringy and useless.

PEACH AND APRICOT FOOL

250 g (8 oz) dried
    apricots, soaked
    overnight in 450 ml
    (¾ pint) water
grated rind and juice
    of 1 lemon
50 g (2 oz) caster
    sugar
3 peaches
2 tablespoons apricot
    brandy
284 ml (10 fl oz)
    double cream,
    whipped

Put the apricots in a saucepan with their soaking water. Add the lemon rind and simmer for 15 to 20 minutes. Drain, reserving 6 tablespoons of the liquid. Cool the apricots and purée in an electric blender or food processor with the reserved liquid, lemon juice and sugar.

Peel and slice the peaches and place in a bowl with the apricot brandy. Stir, then leave to soak for 30 minutes. Reserve 6 peach slices for decoration.

Divide the remaining peach slices between 6 tall glasses. Fold the juice into the apricot purée with three quarters of the cream. Spoon the apricot mixture over the peaches.

Pipe the remaining cream in swirls on top of the fools and decorate with the reserved peach slices.

Serves 6

CRUNCHY APPLE WHIP

125 g (4 oz) ginger
    snaps, crushed
50 g (2 oz) chopped,
    roasted hazelnuts
3 tablespoons clear
    honey
grated rind and juice
    of 1 lemon
500 g (1 lb) cooking
    apples, peeled,
    cored and sliced
1 egg white
25 g (1 oz) caster
    sugar
142 ml (5 fl oz)
    double cream,
    whipped

Mix together the ginger snaps and hazelnuts; set aside.

Put the honey, lemon rind and juice, and apples in a pan. Cover and simmer gently for 10 minutes until the apples are soft. Sieve and leave to cool.

Whisk the egg white until stiff, then whisk in the sugar. Fold into the apple purée with the cream. Divide half the fruit between 6 tall glasses and cover with half the biscuit mixture. Repeat these layers, finishing with a layer of biscuit mixture. Chill before serving.

Serves 6

Peach and Apricot Fool; Crunchy Apple Whip; Apricot Cream Layer

PETITS POTS AU CHOCOLAT

*125 g (4 oz) plain
chocolate, broken
into pieces*
600 ml (1 pint) milk
2 eggs
2 egg yolks
*2 tablespoons caster
sugar*
*whipped cream to
serve (optional)*

*Petits Pots au
Chocolat; Syllabub*

Place the chocolate in a pan with the milk. Simmer gently for 2 minutes, stirring occasionally. Beat together the eggs, yolks and sugar, then pour on the chocolate milk; blend well.

Strain into individual ovenproof pots or ramekins. Place in a roasting pan containing 2.5 cm (1 inch) water. Bake in a preheated moderate oven, 180°C (350°F), Gas Mark 4, for 35 to 40 minutes until just set.

Cool and chill before serving, topped with whipped cream if preferred.
Serves 4 to 6

SYLLABUB

*grated rind and juice
of 1 lemon*
*120 ml (4 fl oz)
white wine*
*75 g (3 oz) caster
sugar*
*284 ml (10 fl oz)
double cream*
1 egg white
*Langue de Chat
biscuits (see page
149) to serve*

Place the lemon rind and juice in a bowl with the wine and half the sugar. Leave to soak for 1 hour.

Whip the cream until it stands in peaks, then gradually add the wine mixture and continue whipping until it holds its shape.

Whisk the egg white until stiff then whisk in the remaining sugar. Carefully fold into the cream mixture. Spoon into individual glasses and serve immediately with Langue de Chat biscuits.
Serves 4

GINGER CREAMS

113 g (4 oz) medium-
  fat curd cheese
1/2 teaspoon ground
  ginger
2 tablespoons coarse-
  cut marmalade
2 tablespoons orange
  juice
1 tablespoon brandy
142 ml (5 fl oz)
  double cream
few slices stem ginger
  to decorate

Place the cheese in a bowl and blend in the ginger, marmalade, orange juice and brandy. Whip the cream until it just holds its shape, then gently fold into the cheese mixture.

Spoon into 4 glass dishes and decorate with ginger. Chill before serving, with Brandy Snaps (see page 148), if liked.
Serves 4

PEACH FRUIT LAYER

175 g (6 oz) medium-
  fat curd cheese
300 g (10 oz) peach
  melba yogurt
3 peaches, stoned and
  sliced
1 tablespoon sherry

Place the cheese in a bowl and blend in the yogurt. Set aside a few peach slices for decoration; mix the remainder with the sherry.

Spoon half the yogurt mixture into 4 tall glasses. Top with the peaches, then cover with the remaining yogurt mixture. Decorate with the reserved peach slices. Serve chilled.
Serves 4

PINEAPPLE CRUNCH

113 g (4 oz) cottage
  cheese with
  pineapple
227 g (8 oz) can
  pineapple slices,
142 ml (5 fl oz)
  double cream,
  whipped
25 g (1 oz) caster
  sugar
3 digestive sweetmeal
  biscuits, crushed
1 tablespoon sesame
  seeds, toasted

Place the cottage cheese in a bowl. Drain the pineapple, chop finely and add to the cheese.

Place a third of the cream in a piping bag fitted with a star nozzle. Fold the remainder into the pineapple mixture with the sugar. Spoon into 4 individual dishes.

Mix together the biscuit crumbs and sesame seeds and sprinkle most of them over the desserts. Pipe a whirl of cream on each and sprinkle with the remaining crumbs. Serve chilled.
Serves 4

Ginger Creams; Peach Fruit Layer; Pineapple Crunch

PRUNE MOUSSE

250 g (8 oz) dried
    prunes
50 g (2 oz)
    muscovado sugar
300 g (10 oz) natural
    yogurt
1 teaspoon lemon
    juice
15 g (½ oz) gelatine,
    soaked in 3 table-
    spoons water
142 ml (5 fl oz) double
    cream, whipped
25 g (1 oz) chopped
    walnuts to decorate

Cover the prunes with water, bring
to the boil and simmer for 20 minutes
until soft. Sieve, or work in an
electric blender with a little of the
cooking liquid until smooth; leave to
cool. Stir in the sugar, yogurt and
lemon juice.

Place the soaked gelatine in a bowl
over a pan of simmering water and
stir until dissolved. Cool slightly,
then fold into the prune mixture with
the cream. Pour into ramekins and
chill until set.

Decorate with the walnuts to serve.
Serves 6

APRICOT WHIP

250 g (8 oz) dried
    apricots, soaked
    overnight
300 g (10 oz) natural
    low-fat yogurt
2 egg whites
2 tablespoons
    muscovado sugar
1 tablespoon flaked
    almonds, roasted

Place the apricots in a pan with the
water in which they were soaked.
Bring to the boil and simmer for
20 minutes until soft. Sieve, or work
in an electric blender with a little of
the cooking liquid until smooth.
Leave to cool then stir in the yogurt.

Whisk the egg whites until stiff,
then whisk in the sugar a little at a
time. Fold into the apricot mixture
and spoon into glasses. Sprinkle with
the almonds and chill until required.
Serves 6

CHESTNUT WHIP

1 × 439 g (15½ oz)
can unsweetened
chestnut purée
50 g (2 oz) soft
brown sugar
4 tablespoons brandy
juice of 1 small
orange
284 ml (10 fl oz)
double cream,
whipped
finely shredded
orange rind to
decorate

Place the chestnut purée and sugar in a bowl and beat until smooth. Mix in the brandy and orange juice, then fold in the cream.

Spoon into glass dishes and decorate with orange rind.
Serves 8

PRUNE WHIP

250 g (8 oz) prunes,
stoned
150 g (5 oz) natural
yogurt
2 tablespoons clear
honey
284 ml (10 fl oz)
double cream,
whipped
2 tablespoons
chopped walnuts to
decorate

Place the prunes in a pan with just enough water to cover and simmer for 15 minutes or until tender. Rub through a sieve or work in an electric blender with 120 ml (4 fl oz) of the cooking water until smooth. Leave to cool.

Fold the prune purée, yogurt and honey into the cream and spoon into individual glass dishes. Decorate with walnuts.
Serves 6 to 8

MANGO FOOL

2 ripe mangoes,
peeled
75 g (3 oz) caster
sugar
284 ml (10 fl oz)
double cream,
whipped
25 g (1 oz) almonds,
toasted, to decorate

Cut as much flesh as possible from each mango. Place the mango flesh and sugar in an electric blender or food processor and work until smooth. Fold the cream into the mango purée.

Spoon into glasses and chill. Top with toasted almonds to serve.
Serves 4

OPPOSITE: *Prune Mousse; Apricot Whip*
RIGHT: *Mint and Apple Whip*

MINT AND APPLE WHIP

750 g (1½ lb)
cooking apples,
peeled and cored
3 tablespoons clear
honey
2 tablespoons water
6 large mint sprigs
5 tablespoons natural
yogurt
2 egg whites
1 tablespoon
muscovado sugar

Slice the apples into a pan and add the honey, water and mint, reserving the top leaves for decoration. Cover and simmer for 10 to 15 minutes; discard the mint. Sieve or work in an electric blender until smooth. Leave to cool then mix in the yogurt.

Whisk the egg whites until stiff, then whisk in the sugar. Fold into the apple mixture. Spoon into individual dishes and decorate with the reserved mint to serve.
Serves 4 to 6

RICH CHOCOLATE MOUSSE

75 g (3 oz) plain chocolate, broken into pieces
3 eggs, separated
2 tablespoons sherry
3 tablespoons whipped cream
chocolate curls to decorate (see note)

Melt the chocolate in a bowl over a pan of hot water, then add the egg yolks and sherry and mix well.

Whisk the egg whites until fairly stiff then carefully fold into the chocolate mixture. Divide between 4 ramekin dishes and leave in the refrigerator to set.

Pipe a cream rosette on each mousse and top with chocolate curls to serve.

Serves 4

NOTE: To make chocolate curls, shave thin layers from a block of chocolate, using a potato peeler.

CHOCOLATE AND ORANGE MOUSSE

125 g (4 oz) plain chocolate, broken into pieces
grated rind and juice of 1 small orange
3 eggs, separated
3 tablespoons double cream, whipped
finely shredded orange rind to decorate

Place the chocolate in a heatproof bowl with the orange rind and juice. Place over a pan of simmering water until melted. Mix in the egg yolks.

Whisk the egg whites until fairly stiff, then fold into the chocolate mixture. Pour into individual glasses and chill until set.

Pipe a rosette of cream on each mousse and decorate with orange rind.

Serves 4 to 6

MOCHA CHARLOTTE

175 g (6 oz) plain chocolate, broken into pieces
450 ml (¾ pint) strong black coffee
2 eggs, separated
50 g (2 oz) caster sugar
15 g (½ oz) gelatine, soaked in 3 tablespoons cold water
426 ml (15 fl oz) double cream, whipped
24 Langue de Chat biscuits (see page 149)
grated chocolate to decorate

Place the chocolate in a small pan with 150 ml (¼ pint) of the coffee. Heat gently until melted, add the remaining coffee and bring to the boil, stirring.

Beat the egg yolks and sugar together until creamy. Stir in the coffee mixture. Return to the pan and stir over a gentle heat until the custard thickens. Add the gelatine and stir until dissolved. Leave to cool.

Stir over a bowl of iced water until the mixture starts to thicken, then fold in two-thirds of the cream. Whisk the egg whites until stiff and fold into the mixture. Turn into a lightly oiled 1.2 litre (2 pint) Charlotte mould and chill until set.

Turn out onto a plate. Cover the sides with a thin layer of cream and press on the biscuits. Top with piped cream and grated chocolate.

Serves 6 to 8

MOUSSE BRAZILIENNE

3 eggs
2 egg yolks
75 g (3 oz) caster sugar
15 g (½ oz) gelatine, soaked in 3 tablespoons strong black coffee
284 ml (10 fl oz) whipping cream, whipped
125 g (4 oz) praline (see below)
CARAMEL:
125 g (4 oz) granulated sugar
4 tablespoons water
4 tablespoons hot strong black coffee

First make the caramel: dissolve the sugar in the water over a gentle heat then cook until a rich brown. Carefully add the hot coffee, all at once, stirring until thoroughly blended; reheat to melt the caramel if necessary, then cool.

Place the eggs, egg yolks and sugar in a bowl and whisk over a pan of hot water until thick and mousse-like.

Place the gelatine and coffee mixture in a bowl over a pan of simmering water and stir until dissolved. Fold into the mousse with the cream and the caramel. Stir over a bowl of iced water until just beginning to set, then add the praline.

Pour into a greased 1.75 litre (3 pint) mould and leave to set. Turn out onto a plate to serve.

Serves 8

Mousse Brazilienne; Mocha Charlotte; Chocolate and Chestnut Mould (see page 120)

TO MAKE PRALINE

Place 50 g (2 oz) blanched almonds and 50 g (2 oz) caster sugar in a heavy-based pan and heat gently until melted. Increase the heat and cook, stirring, until the mixture is nut brown. Turn onto an oiled baking sheet and leave until hard. Crush with a rolling pin and use as required.

GOOSEBERRY MOUSSE

500 g (1 lb)
  gooseberries
3 tablespoons water
175 g (6 oz) caster
  sugar
2 heads of
  elderflower, tied in
  muslin (optional)
2 eggs
1 egg yolk
15 g (1/2 oz) gelatine,
  soaked in 3 table-
  spoons cold water
142 ml (5 fl oz)
  whipping cream,
  whipped
TO DECORATE:
120 ml (4 fl oz)
  double cream,
  whipped
1 kiwi fruit, sliced

Place the gooseberries in a pan with the water, half the sugar and the elderflower, if using. Cover and cook gently for 10 to 15 minutes, until soft. Remove the elderflower and leave to cool. Purée in an electric blender or food processor, then sieve to remove the tops and tails.

Place the eggs, egg yolk and remaining sugar in a bowl and beat with an electric whisk until thick and mousse-like.

Heat the gelatine gently until dissolved. Mix into the gooseberry purée and cool slightly. Carefully fold into the egg mixture with the whipping cream. Turn into a glass bowl and chill until set.

Decorate with piped cream and kiwi fruit slices.

Serves 8

DAMSON MOUSSE

500 g (1 lb) damsons
4 tablespoons water
250 g (8 oz) caster
  sugar
2 eggs
1 egg yolk
15 g (1/2 oz) gelatine,
  soaked in 3 table-
  spoons cold water
284 ml (10 fl oz)
  whipping cream,
  whipped
4 tablespoons double
  cream, whipped, to
  decorate

Place the damsons in a pan with the water and half the sugar. Cover and cook gently for 15 minutes, until tender. Cool slightly, remove the stones, then purée in an electric blender or food processor. Sieve to remove the skins. Leave to cool.

Place the eggs, egg yolk and remaining sugar in a bowl and beat with an electric whisk until thick and mousse-like.

Heat the gelatine gently until dissolved. Mix into the damson purée. When it is just beginning to set, carefully fold into the egg mixture with the whipping cream.

Turn into a 1.2 litre (2 pint) ring mould and chill until set. Turn out onto a serving plate and decorate with piped cream.

Serves 8

BRAMBLE MOUSSE

350 g (12 oz) blackberries
1 tablespoon water
2 eggs
1 egg yolk
75 g (3 oz) caster sugar
15 g (½ oz) gelatine, soaked in 3 tablespoons cold water
284 ml (10 fl oz) double cream, or imitation cream, lightly whipped

Set aside a few blackberries. Place the rest in a pan with the water and simmer gently for 5 minutes. Cool slightly, then transfer to an electric blender or food processor and work until smooth. Sieve to remove pips.

Place the eggs, egg yolk and sugar in a bowl and whisk until thick and mousse-like.

Heat the gelatine gently until dissolved, then fold into the egg mousse with the blackberry purée and half the cream.

Turn into a 1.2 litre (2 pint) glass dish and chill until set. Whip the remaining cream until thick. Decorate the mousse with piped cream rosettes and blackberries.
Serves 6 to 8

COFFEE AND WALNUT MOUSSE

1 tablespoon coffee granules
2 tablespoons boiling water
4 egg yolks
50 g (2 oz) soft light brown sugar
50 g (2 oz) walnuts, finely ground
142 ml (5 fl oz) whipping cream, whipped
TO DECORATE:
4 teaspoons Tia Maria (optional)
4 walnut halves

Blend the coffee granules with the boiling water in a mixing bowl. Add the egg yolks, sugar and walnuts and place the bowl over a pan of simmering water. Whisk until creamy and thick enough to leave a trail.

Remove from the pan and continue whisking until the mixture is cold and thick enough to hold its shape. Fold in the cream.

Spoon into individual serving dishes and top each with a teaspoonful of Tia Maria, if using, and half a walnut. Serve chilled.
Serves 4

CHOCOLATE AND PEPPERMINT MOUSSE

284 ml (10 fl oz) whipping cream, well chilled
½ teaspoon peppermint essence
¼ teaspoon green food colouring (optional)
2 egg whites
1 tablespoon icing or caster sugar
24 chocolate mint sticks, chopped

Pour the cream into a bowl and add the essence, colouring if using, egg whites and sugar. Whisk until stiff enough to stand in peaks and at least doubled in volume. Fold in the chopped chocolate mint sticks.

Spoon into individual freezerproof serving dishes and place in a freezer for about 2 hours, until well chilled and just on the point of freezing. Serve immediately.
Serves 4 to 6

PREPARING MOULDS

For mousses which are to be moulded and turned out, rinse the mould with cold water before filling.

To turn out a moulded mousse, loosen the edge of the mould with the fingertips and dip into a bowl of hand-hot water. If the mould is metal, take it out immediately; if china, count slowly to ten before doing so. Place a plate over the mould, invert and shake once or twice to release.

DAMSON MERINGUE MOUSSE

1 × 397 g (14 oz) can damsons
1 envelope gelatine, dissolved in 2 tablespoons water
1 × 170 g (6 oz) can evaporated milk
3 tablespoons lemon juice
2 egg whites
50 g (2 oz) caster sugar
TO DECORATE:
3-4 tablespoons double cream, whipped
pistachio nuts or toasted slivered almonds

Drain the juice from the damsons and make up to 200 ml (⅓ pint) with warm water. Stir in the dissolved gelatine. Sieve the damsons to remove the stones and stir the purée into the fruit juice. Chill until beginning to thicken.

Pour the evaporated milk into a large mixing bowl. Add the lemon juice and whisk until thick and creamy. Stir in the thickened fruit juice mixture and leave until just beginning to set.

Whisk the egg whites until stiff, then gradually whisk in the sugar to make a soft meringue. Carefully fold into the fruit mixture. Turn into a dampened 1.2 litre (2 pint) mould or individual dishes and chill overnight.

Turn out onto a serving plate and decorate with piped cream and nuts.
Serves 6

OPPOSITE: *Gooseberry Mousse; Damson Mousse*

COFFEE CRÈME CARAMEL

75 g (3 oz)
  granulated sugar
1 tablespoon water
3 eggs
25 g (1 oz) caster
  sugar
450 ml (¾ pint)
  milk
1 tablespoon instant
  coffee powder

Place the granulated sugar and water in a small heavy-based pan. Heat gently until the sugar has completely dissolved. Increase the heat and boil rapidly until a deep brown caramel forms. Pour immediately into 8 buttered ramekin dishes, or a 900 ml (1½ pint) mould. Leave to cool.

Whisk the eggs and caster sugar in a bowl. Heat the milk until warm, stir in the coffee powder and whisk into the eggs. Strain and pour into the moulds. Place in a roasting pan containing enough warm water to come almost to the top of the dishes.

Bake in a preheated moderate oven, 160°C (325°F), Gas Mark 3, for 40 to 45 minutes for individual crème caramels, about 1 hour for a large one, or until set.

Leave until cold then turn onto a serving dish(es). Serve with cream.
Serves 4 to 8

CRÈME BRÛLÉE

4 egg yolks
1 tablespoon caster
  sugar
2 × 284 ml (10 fl oz)
  cartons double
  cream
few drops of vanilla
  essence
TO FINISH:
50 g (2 oz) caster
  sugar

Beat the egg yolks and sugar together. Warm the cream in a double saucepan, or bowl over a pan of simmering water. Carefully stir in the egg mixture. Continue cooking gently, stirring constantly, until thickened enough to coat the back of a spoon. Add the vanilla essence.

Strain into 6 ramekin dishes and place in a roasting pan, containing 2.5 cm (1 inch) water. Place in a preheated cool oven, 140°C (275°F), Gas Mark 1, for 30 to 40 minutes.

Remove dishes from the pan, cool then chill in refrigerator overnight.

To finish: sprinkle evenly with sugar. Place under a preheated hot grill until the sugar has caramelized. Cool, then chill in the refrigerator for 2 hours before serving.
Serves 6

RATAFIA CRÈME BRÛLÉE

6 egg yolks
2 × 284 ml (10 fl oz)
  cartons double
  cream
½ teaspoon almond
  essence
1 × 85 g (3 oz)
  packet ratafia
  biscuits, finely
  crushed
75 g (3 oz) caster
  sugar

Whisk the egg yolks in a bowl. Heat the cream gently to just below boiling point and stir into the egg yolks. Place the bowl over a pan of simmering water or pour the cream mixture into the top of a double saucepan. Heat gently until the mixture thickens, but do not boil.

When the mixture is thick enough to coat the back of a spoon, remove from the heat and stir in the essence. Pour into 6 or 8 ramekin dishes. Cool, then chill overnight.

Cover with the crushed ratafias, then with sugar. Place under a moderately hot grill until the sugar melts and caramelizes. Cool, then chill for 2 to 3 hours before serving.
Serves 6 or 8

ABOVE: *Crème Brûlée*
OPPOSITE: *Atholl Brose; Apricot Ambrosia; Crème Caramel*

ATHOLL BROSE

40 g (1½ oz)
    almonds, chopped
40 g (1½ oz)
    medium oatmeal
284 ml (10 fl oz)
    double cream
1 tablespoon lemon
    juice
4 tablespoons whisky
3 tablespoons honey
lemon twists to
    decorate

Place the almonds and oatmeal under a preheated medium grill until brown, turning frequently. Leave to cool.

Whip the cream until it stands in soft peaks, then whisk in the lemon juice, whisky and honey.

Fold in the almonds and oatmeal. Spoon into 6 glasses and chill. Decorate with lemon twists before serving.

Serves 6

APRICOT AMBROSIA

1 × 411 g (14½ oz)
    can apricot halves
1 tablespoon honey
50 g (2 oz) ratafias
142 ml (5 fl oz)
    double cream,
    whipped
1 tablespoon flaked
    almonds, toasted

Drain the apricots and place in an electric blender with the honey. Work until smooth.

Break the ratafias into bite-sized pieces. Fold into the whipped cream, together with the apricot purée.

Spoon into 4 glass dishes and chill. Sprinkle with almonds to serve.

Serves 4

CRÈME CARAMEL

75 g (3 oz)
    granulated sugar
3 tablespoons water
3 eggs
25 g (1 oz) caster
    sugar
450 ml (¾ pint)
    milk
½ teaspoon vanilla
    essence

Put the granulated sugar and water in a pan. Heat gently, stirring, until dissolved, then cook to a rich caramel without stirring. Carefully add 1 teaspoon of boiling water and pour into a 900 ml (1½ pint) soufflé dish or mould. Leave to set.

Beat the eggs and caster sugar together. Heat the milk almost to boiling point and add to the eggs with the vanilla essence. Mix well. Strain into the soufflé dish and place in a roasting pan containing 2.5 cm (1 inch) water. Bake in a preheated cool oven, 140°C (275°F), Gas Mark 1, for 1½ hours until set. Cool, then turn out onto a serving dish.

Serves 4

CHEESECAKES AND MERINGUES

This chapter combines two of the best known types of desserts. Both of them can be made with an infinite variety of flavourings, fillings and toppings. Cheesecakes have become universally popular, served as mid-morning treats and teatime gâteaux, as well as delicious desserts.

Baked cheesecakes are usually heavier and richer than the uncooked gelatine-set type, which are sometimes known as American cheesecakes. Lemon is the flavour most often associated with cheesecakes, but there are many alternatives to choose from. Try a creamy chocolate cheesecake or a ginger-flavoured one, for a change. Cheesecake bases can also be varied. The biscuit crumb is the most frequent choice; pastry and sponge bases are more usual in the traditional baked cheesecakes. The toppings can provide endless variety. Fresh fruit looks most attractive – choose soft fruit in summer, citrus fruit in winter.

Like cheesecakes, meringues have the advantage that they can be made in advance. Here you will find both traditional and new ideas for mouth-watering meringue desserts, including Pavlova, vacherins, meringue baskets and meringue pies. In addition there are handy hints on obtaining the best results with meringue mixtures. Except perhaps for slimmers, these sweet desserts are usually favourites with all of the family – Baked Alaska (page 85) always goes down a treat, for example. For special occasions choose from the attractive meringue baskets, elaborate cream-filled gâteaux and vacherins.

CHOCOLATE CHEESECAKE

50 g (2 oz) butter,
  melted
150 g (5 oz)
  digestive biscuits,
  finely crushed
50 g (2 oz) demerara
  sugar
175 g (6 oz) plain
  chocolate
1 × 227 g (8 oz)
  carton cream cheese
75 g (3 oz) caster
  sugar
2 eggs, separated
284 ml (10 fl oz)
  double cream,
  lightly whipped
chocolate curls to
  decorate (see note)

Combine the butter, biscuit crumbs and demerara sugar. Press the mixture over the base and sides of a greased 23 cm (9 inch) loose-bottomed flan tin and place in the refrigerator to harden.

Melt the chocolate in a bowl over a pan of hot water. Blend the cheese, caster sugar and egg yolks together, then mix in the chocolate. Fold in half the cream.

Whisk the egg whites until stiff and fold into the mixture. Turn into the crumb case and leave in the refrigerator to set.

Whip the cream until stiff enough to pipe. Decorate the cheesecake with cream and chocolate curls.

Serves 6

NOTE: To make chocolate curls, shave thin layers from a block of chocolate, using a potato peeler.

BAKED CINNAMON CHEESECAKE

150 g (5 oz) plain
  flour
75 g (3 oz) butter
40 g (1½ oz) caster
  sugar
227 g (8 oz) packet
  creamy soft cheese
227 g (8 oz) curd
  cheese
50 g (2 oz) soft light
  brown sugar
142 ml (5 fl oz)
  soured cream
2 teaspoons ground
  cinnamon
4 eggs
TO DECORATE:
whipped cream
ground cinnamon

Sift the flour into a bowl. Rub in the butter and sugar until the mixture resembles breadcrumbs. Press into a stiff dough and knead until smooth.

Soften the cream cheese in a bowl. Beat in the curd cheese and sugar, then stir in the cream and cinnamon. Whisk in the eggs, one at a time.

Place the shortbread in a lined and greased deep 20 cm (8 inch) loose-bottomed cake tin. Press firmly with the knuckles to cover base and sides completely. Pour in the mixture. Bake in a preheated moderate oven, 160°C (325°F), Gas Mark 3, for 1 hour, until set. Leave in the tin until cold.

Turn out, decorate with cream and sprinkle lightly with cinnamon.

Serves 8

BAKED CHEESECAKE

A quick recipe for those with a food processor.

50 g (2 oz) butter,
  melted
250 g (8 oz)
  digestive biscuits
227 g (8 oz) cottage
  cheese
200 g (7 oz) full fat
  soft cheese
125 g (4 oz) caster
  sugar
3 eggs, separated
25 g (1 oz) cornflour
½ teaspoon vanilla
  essence
142 ml (5 fl oz)
  soured cream

Fit the metal chopping blade and process the butter and biscuits together. Press onto the base of a well greased 20 cm (8 inch) loose-bottomed cake tin.

Place the cheeses in the processor bowl and process until blended. Add the remaining ingredients, except the egg whites, and process until blended. Whisk the egg whites until stiff and fold in.

Pour onto the biscuit base and bake in a preheated cool oven, 150°C (300°F), Gas Mark 2, for 1½ hours. Turn off the heat and leave the oven door ajar. Leave the cheesecake in the oven until cold.

Carefully push out of the tin and slide onto a serving plate.

Makes one 20 cm (8 inch) cake

BLACKCURRANT AND ORANGE CHEESECAKE

50 g (2 oz)
  margarine, melted
125 g (4 oz)
  digestive biscuits,
  crushed
25 g (1 oz) demerara
  sugar
300 g (10 oz) curd
  cheese
50 g (2 oz) caster
  sugar
2 eggs, separated
grated rind and juice
  of 1/2 orange
15 g (1/2 oz) gelatine
284 ml (10 fl oz)
  whipping cream,
  whipped
TOPPING:
1 × 213 g (7 1/2 oz)
  can blackcurrants
2 teaspoons arrowroot
finely grated rind and
  juice of 1 orange

Combine the margarine, biscuit crumbs and demerara sugar. Spread the mixture over the base of an oiled 20 cm (8 inch) loose-bottomed cake tin and chill until firm.

Place the cheese in a bowl and beat in the sugar, egg yolks and orange rind. Soak the gelatine in the orange juice, then heat gently until dissolved. Stir into the cheese mixture with the cream.

Whisk the egg whites until stiff. Fold 2 tablespoons into the mixture to soften it. Fold in the remaining egg white and spread evenly over the biscuit base. Chill until set.

Drain the currants and heat the syrup. Blend the arrowroot with the orange rind and juice, then pour on the syrup, stirring. Return to the pan and bring to the boil, stirring, until thick. Add the currants and cool.

Remove cheesecake from the tin and spread over the topping.

Serves 8

GINGER CHEESECAKE

75 g (3 oz) butter
175 g (6 oz)
  digestive biscuits,
  crushed
1 tablespoon ground
  ginger
FILLING:
227 g (8 oz) medium-
  fat curd cheese
2 tablespoons natural
  yogurt
2 eggs, separated
2 tablespoons soft
  brown sugar
2 pieces stem ginger,
  finely chopped
1 tablespoon ginger
  syrup (from jar)
grated nutmeg
TO DECORATE:
142 ml (5 fl oz)
  double cream
stem ginger slices

Melt the butter in a pan. Remove from the heat and mix in the biscuit crumbs and ginger. Press into the base and sides of a 20 cm (8 inch) flan dish.

To make the filling, place the cheese in a bowl and blend in the yogurt, egg yolks and sugar. Stir in the ginger and syrup. Whisk the egg whites until stiff and fold into the cheese mixture. Pour into the flan case and sprinkle with grated nutmeg.

Bake in a preheated moderate oven, 160°C (325°F), Gas Mark 3, for 25 to 35 minutes until firm and golden. Allow to cool, then chill.

Whip the cream until thick. Decorate the cheesecake with piped whipped cream and ginger slices before serving.

Serves 6

TYPES OF CHEESE

Cheesecakes can be made with an endless variety of textures, flavours and toppings. Baked cheesecakes are usually richer and have a heavier texture than the gelatine-set ones. Cheese – usually soft – is the essential ingredient in all cheesecakes. There are several kinds of soft cheese and the type used will determine the richness and texture of the cheesecake.

Full fat soft cheese contains about 80% milk fat and gives a rich cheesecake. The variety sold in foil-wrapped blocks is most suitable in baked cheesecakes.

Curd cheese is a medium-fat soft cheese with a high moisture content. It is excellent used in most cheesecakes but it does not have a long shelf life and should be used soon after purchase.

Cottage cheese is a low-fat curd cheese containing less than 2% milk fat. It will yield a light-textured cheesecake and is best sieved before combining with other ingredients.

OPPOSITE: *Baked Cinnamon Cheesecake*
RIGHT: *Ginger Cheesecake*

Baked Cheesecake with Sultanas

BAKED CHEESECAKE WITH SULTANAS

75 g (3 oz) butter
125 g (4 oz) caster
    sugar
grated rind and juice
    of 1 lemon
300 g (10 oz) curd
    cheese
2 eggs, separated
50 g (2 oz) ground
    almonds
25 g (1 oz) semolina
50 g (2 oz) sultanas
sifted icing sugar for
    dredging

Cream the butter, sugar and lemon rind together until light and fluffy. Beat in the cheese gradually, then mix in the egg yolks and beat thoroughly. Add the almonds, semolina, sultanas and lemon juice and mix well. Whisk the egg whites until stiff and carefully fold into the cheese mixture.

Spoon into a lined and greased 20 cm (8 inch) loose-bottomed cake tin and bake in a preheated moderate oven, 180°C (350°F), Gas Mark 4 for 50 to 60 minutes. Turn off the heat and leave the cheesecake in the oven until cold. Turn out and sprinkle with icing sugar to serve.
Serves 6 to 8

CHILLED RASPBERRY CHEESECAKE

50 g (2 oz) butter
125 g (4 oz)
    digestive biscuits,
    crushed
227 g (8 oz) medium-
    fat curd cheese
113 g (4 oz) cottage
    cheese, sieved
75 g (3 oz) caster
    sugar
finely grated rind and
    juice of 1 lemon
15 g (1/2 oz) gelatine
2 tablespoons water
284 ml (10 fl oz)
    double cream,
    whipped
3 egg whites
175 g (6 oz)
    raspberries

Melt the butter in a pan. Remove from the heat and mix in the biscuit crumbs. Press into the base of an oiled 20 cm (8 inch) loose-bottomed cake tin. Chill in the refrigerator to harden.

Place the cheeses in a bowl and blend in the sugar, lemon rind and juice. Soak the gelatine in the water, then place the bowl over a pan of gently simmering water and stir until the gelatine has dissolved. Cool slightly, then stir into the cheese mixture. Fold in half of the cream.

Whisk the egg whites until stiff and fold in. Pour the filling over the biscuit base. Chill in the refrigerator until firm.

Carefully remove the cheesecake from the tin and place on a serving plate. Decorate with the remaining whipped cream and the raspberries.
Serves 8
NOTE: If fresh raspberries are not available, use frozen ones or a can of raspberry pie filling for the topping.

FREEZING CHEESECAKES

Most cheesecakes freeze well, whether they are the cooked or gelatine-set variety, and because they are so popular they are an excellent dessert to keep on standby in the freezer. Best results are obtained if the cheesecake is frozen without its topping. Open freeze the cooled or chilled cheesecake – in its greased loose-bottomed cake tin – until solid. Remove the cheesecake from the tin, wrap in aluminium foil and place in a freezer bag. Seal, label and freeze for up to 1 month.

To thaw, unwrap and place the frozen cheesecake on a serving plate. Leave baked cheesecakes overnight at room temperature and gelatine-set cheesecakes to thaw in the refrigerator overnight. Alternatively if you need to thaw a cheesecake quickly, remove wrappings and leave at room temperature. A baked cheesecake will take about 4 hours; a gelatine-set one will take 2 to 3 hours.

OPPOSITE: *Baked Blackcurrant Cheesecake; Chocolate Mint Cheesecake*

BAKED BLACKCURRANT CHEESECAKE

40 g (1½ oz) butter
75 g (3 oz) digestive
  biscuits, crushed
113 g (4 oz) medium-
  fat curd cheese
50 g (2 oz) cottage
  cheese, sieved
5 tablespoons
  blackcurrant
  yogurt
2 eggs, separated
1 tablespoon cornflour
finely grated rind of
  ½ lemon
40 g (1½ oz) caster
  sugar
TOPPING:
142 ml (5 fl oz)
  soured cream
½ × 397 g (14 oz)
  can blackcurrant
  pie filling
whipped cream
  (optional)

Melt the butter in a pan and stir in the biscuit crumbs. Press into the base of an oiled 18-20 cm (7-8 inch) loose-bottomed cake tin. Chill in the refrigerator to harden.

Place the cheeses in a bowl and blend in the yogurt, egg yolks, cornflour and lemon rind. Whisk the egg whites until stiff, fold in the sugar, then fold into the cheese mixture. Spoon over the biscuit base and bake in a preheated moderate oven, 180°C (350°F), Gas Mark 4, for 35 to 45 minutes or until firm.

Remove the cheesecake from the oven and spread the soured cream over the top. Return to the oven for 5 minutes. Cool in the tin.

Carefully remove the cheesecake from the tin and place on a serving plate. Spread the blackcurrant pie filling over the top and decorate with cream if wished. Serve chilled.
Serves 4 to 6

CHOCOLATE MINT CHEESECAKE

50 g (2 oz) butter
125 g (4 oz)
  chocolate digestive
  biscuits, crushed
125 g (4 oz) plain
  chocolate, melted
4 tablespoons milk
2 × 62.5 g (2.2 oz)
  packets soft cream
  cheese
113 g (4 oz) cottage
  cheese, sieved
50 g (2 oz) caster
  sugar
½ teaspoon
  peppermint essence
½ teaspoon vanilla
  essence
15 g (½ oz) gelatine
142 ml (5 fl oz)
  double cream,
  whipped
chocolate mints to
  decorate

Melt the butter in a pan. Remove from the heat and stir in the biscuit crumbs. Mix well and press into the base of an oiled 18-20 cm (7-8 inch) loose-bottomed cake tin. Chill in the refrigerator to harden.

Melt the chocolate with the milk in a bowl over a pan of hot water. Place the cheeses in a bowl and blend in the sugar, essences and chocolate. Soak the gelatine in 4 tablespoons water, then place the bowl over a pan of simmering water to dissolve. Cool slightly and stir into the chocolate mixture.

Fold half of the cream into the filling. Spoon over the biscuit base and chill in the refrigerator until firm.

Carefully remove the cheesecake from the tin and place on a serving plate. Decorate with the reserved cream and chocolate mints.
Serves 6 to 8

ORANGE CHEESECAKE

50 g (2 oz) butter
50 g (2 oz) soft dark
  brown sugar
175 g (6 oz)
  digestive biscuits,
  crushed
227 g (8 oz) packet
  creamy soft cheese
227 g (8 oz) curd
  cheese
2 eggs, separated
142 ml (5 fl oz)
  soured cream
25 g (1 oz) caster
  sugar
grated rind and juice
  of 1 orange
1 envelope gelatine,
  dissolved in 2
  tablespoons water
2-3 tablespoons
  orange Curaçao
TO DECORATE:
142 ml (5 fl oz)
  double cream
½ orange, sliced

Melt the butter and stir in the brown sugar and biscuit crumbs. Press onto the base of a 23 cm (9 inch) loose-bottomed flan tin or cake tin. Chill until firm.

Mix together the cheeses in a mixing bowl, then beat in the egg yolks, soured cream and caster sugar. Stir in the orange rind and juice, dissolved gelatine and Curaçao. Leave until just on the point of setting, then fold in the stiffly whisked egg whites.

Pour onto the biscuit base and chill until firm. Decorate with piped whipped cream and orange slices.
Serves 6 to 8

BLENDER CHEESECAKE

125 g (4 oz)
  digestive biscuits
25 g (1 oz) demerara
  sugar
50 g (2 oz) butter or
  margarine, melted
340 g (12 oz) cottage
  cheese
50 g (2 oz) caster
  sugar
grated rind and juice
  of 1 lemon
2 eggs, separated
284 ml (10 fl oz)
  single cream
15 g (½ oz) gelatine
TO FINISH:
125 g (4 oz)
  strawberries or
  raspberries
142 ml (5 fl oz)
  double cream,
  whipped

Break the biscuits into pieces and place in an electric blender. Blend on maximum speed for 20 seconds. Combine the crumbs, demerara sugar and butter. Spread over the base of a 20 cm (8 inch) loose-bottomed cake tin and chill until firm.

Place the cheese in the blender with the caster sugar, lemon rind and juice, egg yolks and cream. Soak the gelatine in 3 tablespoons cold water, then heat gently until dissolved. Pour into the blender and blend on maximum speed for 30 seconds. Turn into a bowl.

Whisk the egg whites until stiff then fold into the cheese mixture. Spoon over the base and chill until set.

Transfer to a serving dish, arrange the fruit on top and pipe the cream around the edge.
Serves 8

QUICK ORANGE CHEESECAKE

50 g (2 oz) butter
125 g (4 oz)
  digestive biscuits,
  crushed
227 g (8 oz) medium-
  fat curd cheese
150 g (5 oz) natural
  yogurt
½ packet orange jelly
3 tablespoons water
1 tablespoon sugar
grated rind and juice
  of 1 orange
1 × 212 g (7½ oz)
  can mandarin
  oranges, drained

Melt the butter in a pan. Remove from the heat and mix in the biscuit crumbs. Press into an oiled 20 cm (8 inch) flan ring placed on a serving plate. Chill until firm.

Blend together the curd cheese and yogurt. Dissolve the jelly in the water over a low heat. Cool slightly, then stir in the sugar, orange rind and juice. Add to the cheese and whisk until smooth. Pour into the flan ring and leave in the refrigerator until set.

Carefully remove the flan ring and decorate the cheesecake with mandarin oranges. Serve chilled.
Serves 4 to 6

LEFT: *Orange Cheesecake*
OPPOSITE: *Lemon and Apple Cheesecake; Kiwi and Gooseberry Cheesecake*

LEMON AND APPLE CHEESECAKE

75 g (3 oz) margarine, melted
250 g (8 oz) ginger snaps, crushed
25 g (1 oz) demerara sugar
250 g (8 oz) cooking apples, peeled, cored and sliced
1 tablespoon water
227 g (8 oz) curd cheese
50 g (2 oz) caster sugar
grated rind and juice of 1 lemon
15 g (½ oz) gelatine, soaked in 3 tablespoons cold water
250 ml (8 fl oz) double cream, whipped
6-8 lemon twists

Combine the margarine, biscuit crumbs and demerara sugar. Press over the base and sides of a 23 cm (9 inch) flan dish. Chill until firm.

Place the apples and water in a pan, cover and simmer gently for 10 to 15 minutes. Work in an electric blender or food processor until smooth; cool.

Place the cheese in a bowl and beat in the caster sugar and lemon rind. Mix the lemon juice into the apple purée and stir into the cheese mixture. Heat the gelatine gently until dissolved then stir into the cheese mixture with two thirds of the cream.

Spoon into the crumb case, smooth the surface and leave in the refrigerator to set.

Decorate with the remaining cream and lemon twists.
Serves 6 to 8

KIWI AND GOOSEBERRY CHEESECAKE

40 g (1½ oz) butter
125 g (4 oz) ginger snaps, crushed
500 g (1 lb) gooseberries
125 g (4 oz) caster sugar
2 heads of elderflower, tied in muslin (optional)
15 g (½ oz) gelatine, soaked in 3 tablespoons cold water
227 g (8 oz) curd cheese
few drops of green food colouring
142 ml (5 fl oz) double cream, whipped
3 kiwi fruit, peeled and thinly sliced

Melt the butter in a pan and stir in the biscuit crumbs. Spread the mixture over the base of a greased 18 cm (7 inch) loose-bottomed cake tin and chill until firm.

Place the gooseberries in a pan with the sugar and elderflower, if using. Cover and simmer for 10 to 15 minutes, until soft. Leave to cool, then remove the elderflower. Sieve or work in an electric blender or food processor until smooth.

Heat the gelatine gently until dissolved; stir into the gooseberry purée. Beat the cheese in a bowl to soften, then mix in the colouring, purée and cream. Turn into the tin and place in the refrigerator to set.

Remove the cheesecake from the tin and place on a serving plate. Arrange overlapping slices of kiwi fruit around the edge to serve.
Serves 6 to 8

ORANGE AND LEMON CREAMS

2 × 62.5 g (2.2 oz) packets soft cream cheese
2 tablespoons natural yogurt
grated rind of ½ orange
grated rind and juice of ½ lemon
1 tablespoon caster sugar
2 small oranges
120 ml (4 fl oz) soured cream
25 g (1 oz) brown sugar
25 g (1 oz) flaked almonds
Sponge fingers (see page 151) to serve

Place the cheese in a bowl and soften with a wooden spoon. Blend in the yogurt, orange rind, lemon rind and juice, and caster sugar. Place in 4 heatproof ramekin dishes.

Peel the oranges and divide into segments, removing all pith. Arrange the orange pieces on top of the cheese mixture.

Stir the soured cream until smooth and spoon over the oranges. Sprinkle with the brown sugar and almonds. Chill in the refrigerator until required.

Place under a preheated moderate grill for 3 to 4 minutes until the sugar melts and the nuts turn brown. Serve immediately, with sponge fingers.
Serves 4

Pashka

MOCHA DESSERT

1 tablespoon custard powder
1 teaspoon coffee granules
1 teaspoon cocoa powder
1½ tablespoons soft brown sugar
300 ml (½ pint) milk
½ teaspoon vanilla essence
113 g (4 oz) medium-fat curd cheese
2 dessert pears, peeled, halved and cored
grated nutmeg
chopped walnuts to decorate

Blend the custard powder, coffee, cocoa and sugar with a little of the milk. Heat the remaining milk until almost boiling, then pour onto the custard mixture, stirring. Return to the heat, stirring, until the custard thickens. Cool slightly and stir in the vanilla essence.

Place the cheese in a bowl and soften with a wooden spoon. Gradually blend in the custard, whisking if necessary, until smooth.

Place the pears in a serving dish and spoon the mocha mixture over. Sprinkle with grated nutmeg and decorate with walnuts. Serve chilled.
Serves 4

PASHKA

2 × 227 g (8 oz) packets creamy soft cheese
1 egg yolk
75 g (3 oz) caster sugar
grated rind and juice of 1 lemon
120 ml (4 fl oz) double cream, whipped
50 g (2 oz) blanched almonds, chopped and browned
50 g (2 oz) glacé cherries, quartered
50 g (2 oz) raisins
25 g (1 oz) flaked almonds, toasted, to decorate

Place the cheese in a bowl with the egg yolk, sugar and lemon rind. Beat together thoroughly until smooth, then stir in the lemon juice. Fold in the cream with the chopped almonds and fruit.

Line a 1 litre (1¾ pint) clay flower pot or pudding basin with a piece of muslin large enough to overlap the top. Spoon in the cheese mixture and fold the cloth over. Cover with a saucer and place a 500 g (1 lb) weight on top. Place in a bowl and chill in the refrigerator overnight.

To serve, unfold the cloth, invert onto a serving plate and remove the muslin. Decorate with the almonds.
Serves 6 to 8

STRAWBERRY CHEESECAKE

50 g (2 oz)
  margarine or
  butter, melted
125 g (4 oz) digestive
  biscuits, crushed
25 g (1 oz)
  muscovado sugar
350 g (12 oz) curd
  cheese
4 tablespoons clear
  honey
150 g (5 oz) natural
  yogurt
grated rind and juice
  of 1 lemon
15 g (½ oz) gelatine,
  soaked in 3 table-
  spoons water
3 egg whites
250 g (8 oz)
  strawberries

Combine the margarine or butter, biscuit crumbs and sugar. Press the mixture over the base of a 20 cm (8 inch) loose-bottomed cake tin and place in the refrigerator for 20 minutes until firm.

Place the cheese in a bowl and mix in the honey, yogurt, lemon rind and juice. Beat until smooth. Place the soaked gelatine in a bowl over a pan of simmering water and stir until dissolved. Stir into the cheese mixture.

Whisk the egg whites until stiff, then fold lightly into the cheese mixture. Spoon over the biscuit base and chill for 2 to 3 hours until set.

Remove the cheesecake from the tin and arrange the strawberries on top.
Serves 6 to 8

CHEESE AND YOGURT CREAMS

227 g (8 oz) cream
  cheese
150 g (5 oz) natural
  yogurt
2 tablespoons clear
  honey
1 egg white
250 g (8 oz)
  strawberries

Place the cheese, yogurt and honey in a bowl and mix well. Whisk the egg white until fairly stiff then fold into the cheese mixture.

Line 6 heart-shaped moulds with muslin, spoon in the cheese mixture and smooth the tops. Place on a plate and leave to drain in the refrigerator for 3 to 4 hours. Turn out onto individual dishes and surround with strawberries.

Alternatively, spoon the cheese mixture into ramekin dishes, arrange the strawberries on top and chill.
Serves 6
NOTE: Other fresh soft fruit can be used in place of strawberries, e.g. raspberries, blackberries, cooked blackcurrants or redcurrants.

Strawberry Cheesecake; Cheese and Yogurt Creams

Croquembouche

MERINGUE ITALIENNE

3 tablespoons water
250 g (8 oz)
   granulated sugar
3 egg whites,
   whisked
½ teaspoon vanilla
   essence

Place the water and sugar in a heavy-based pan over low heat until the sugar has dissolved and the liquid is clear. Increase the heat and boil rapidly until 150°C (298°F) registers on a sugar thermometer, or until a small amount, dropped into cold water, can be rolled into a hard ball.

Pour the syrup into the stiffly whisked egg whites in a slow thin stream, whisking constantly, to form a thick glossy meringue. Whisk in the vanilla essence.

Meringue Italienne is similar to an American frosting and should have the consistency of whipped cream. Use as a cake filling or topping, or on trifles.

This quantity is sufficient to fill and ice the top of a 20 cm (8 inch) cake.

MERINGUE SUISSE

4 egg whites
250 g (8 oz) caster
   sugar
1 teaspoon lemon
   juice

Whisk the egg whites in a large bowl until very stiff and dry; if the meringue slides around the bowl when tilted, carry on whisking.

When the egg whites are stiff enough, add the sugar 1 tablespoon at a time, whisking very thoroughly between each addition. Finally, whisk in the lemon juice. The meringue should be smooth, glossy and form soft peaks.

For a more open-textured meringue, whisk in half the sugar and fold in the remainder with a metal spoon.

Use immediately to make shells, rounds or baskets; on pies and puddings; in mousses and ice creams.

This quantity will make: about 72 × 2.5 cm (1 inch) shells; 8 to 12 × 7.5 cm (3 inch) baskets; 1 × 20 cm (8 inch) basket, vacherin or Pavlova circle; 3 × 20 cm (8 inch) flat circles.

MERINGUE CUITE

4 egg whites
250 g (8 oz) icing
   sugar, sifted
½ teaspoon vanilla
   essence

Place the ingredients in a large mixing bowl over a pan of simmering water. Whisk with a rotary or wire whisk for about 10 minutes, until the mixture is very thick and glossy and forms soft but well-shaped peaks.

Remove the bowl from the heat and continue whisking until the bowl is cool enough to touch; the heat from the bowl may crystallize the sugar, so whisk thoroughly.

Meringue Cuite gives a much more defined shape than Meringue Suisse and retains its form much longer.

Use as for Meringue Suisse (see right); quantities are the same.

CROQUEMBOUCHE

MERINGUE SHELLS:
4 egg whites
*250 g (8 oz) caster
   sugar*
*1 teaspoon lemon
   juice*
*caster sugar for
   sprinkling*
FILLING:
*284 ml (10 fl oz)
   whipping cream*
*1 tablespoon kirsch
   (optional)*
*250 g (8 oz) black
   cherries, stoned*

Prepare the meringue as for Meringue Suisse (see opposite). Using a large piping bag fitted with a 1 cm (½ inch) plain or star nozzle and baking sheets lined with silicone paper, pipe one third into shells about 2.5 cm (1 inch) in diameter, a third slightly larger, and a third into shells about 3.5 cm (1½ inches) across. There should be about 16 of each size. Sprinkle lightly with sugar.

Place in a very cool oven, 120°C (250°F), Gas Mark ½, for 2 hours or until firm. Remove the paper, turn upside down and return to the oven for 1 to 1½ hours to dry.

Whip the cream with the kirsch, if using, until stiff.

Arrange some of the larger meringue shells in a 20 cm (8 inch) circle on a serving plate. Pipe a rosette of cream between each. Arrange the remaining shells, with the cherries in between, on top in progressively smaller circles to form a pyramid, using cream to hold the shape.

Serves 6

TIPS ON MAKING MERINGUES

Meringue is made from a mixture of whisked egg white and sugar. There are three types of meringue: Meringue Suisse, Meringue Cuite and Meringue Italienne. They are quite different, but there are some basic rules.

All meringues should be prepared in a large, very clean, dry mixing bowl. This enables the maximum amount of air to be incorporated to produce the greatest volume. Any grease or egg yolk will prevent the egg white from whisking. The egg whites should be at room temperature.

Meringue Suisse is the most frequently prepared meringue, made simply by whisking in 50 g (2 oz) caster sugar to each egg white. It does, however, deteriorate fairly quickly after preparation and should be used immediately, whereas Meringue Cuite and Meringue Italienne hold their shape for several hours. Meringues are best cooked on silicone or rice paper, but if neither is available use thoroughly oiled baking sheets.

PAVLOVA

4 egg whites
*250 g (8 oz) caster
   sugar*
*1 tablespoon
   cornflour*
2 teaspoons vinegar
*¼ teaspoon vanilla
   essence*
FILLING:
*284 ml (10 fl oz)
   double cream*
2 bananas, sliced
*1 small pineapple,
   cut into cubes*
*2 passion fruit, peeled
   and sliced*
*2 peaches, peeled and
   sliced*

Whisk the egg whites until stiff. Add the sugar, a tablespoon at a time, whisking until the meringue is very stiff. Whisk in the cornflour, vinegar and vanilla.

Pile the meringue onto a baking sheet lined with silicone paper and spread into a 23 cm (9 inch) round. Hollow out the centre slightly and bake in a preheated cool oven, 150°C (300°F), Gas Mark 2, for 1½ hours.

Cool, then remove the paper and place the pavlova on a serving dish. Whip the cream until stiff and fold in some of the fruit. Pile into the pavlova and decorate with the remaining fruit.

Serves 6 to 8

Pavlova, topped with tropical fruit

ITALIAN-STYLE TRIFLE

4 trifle sponges
2 tablespoons sherry
    (optional)
1 × 439 g (15½ oz)
    can pineapple
    pieces
300 ml (½ pint) cold
    custard or Vanilla
    Cream Sauce (see
    page 153)
MERINGUE TOPPING:
3 egg whites
175 g (6 oz) caster
    sugar
½ teaspoon vanilla
    essence

Crumble the trifle sponges into an ovenproof serving dish. Sprinkle with the sherry, if using. Drain the pineapple and sprinkle half of the juice over the cake. Arrange the pineapple pieces on top and pour over the custard or Vanilla Cream Sauce.

Prepare the meringue as for Meringue Suisse (see page 82) and spoon it over the custard or Vanilla Cream Sauce. Place in a preheated moderately hot oven, 200°C (400°F), Gas Mark 6, for 3 to 4 minutes until just the tips of the meringue are golden brown.

Serve warm or cold.
Serves 6 to 8

BAKED ALASKA

1 × 15-18 cm
    (6-7 inch) sponge
    flan case
250 g (8 oz)
    strawberries, sliced
    (optional)
⅓-½ litre
    (¾-1 pint) straw-
    berry ice cream
MERINGUE TOPPING:
4 egg whites
250 g (8 oz) caster
    sugar
½ teaspoon vanilla
    essence
TO DECORATE:
25-50 g (1-2 oz)
    flaked almonds
    (optional)
caster sugar

Place the flan case on an ovenproof plate and arrange the strawberries on the base, if using. Spoon the ice cream over the top. Place in the freezer or freezing compartment of the refrigerator while making the meringue topping, as in Meringue Suisse (see page 82).

Working as quickly as possible, pile the meringue onto the prepared base, completely enclosing the ice cream. Stick the almonds into the meringue, if using, and sprinkle lightly with a little caster sugar. Place immediately in a preheated hot oven, 200°C (400°F), Gas Mark 6, for 3 to 4 minutes or until the meringue peaks are lightly browned. Serve immediately.
Serves 6

LEFT: *Italian-style Trifle; Pineapple Meringue Pie*
OPPOSITE: *Baked Alaska*

PINEAPPLE MERINGUE PIE

50 g (2 oz) cornflour
450 ml (¾ pint)
  pineapple juice
3 eggs, separated
25 g (1 oz) butter
175 g (6 oz) caster
  sugar
caster sugar for
  sprinkling
Vanilla Cream Sauce
  (see page 153) to
  serve
SHORTCRUST
  PASTRY:
175 g (6 oz) plain
  flour
pinch of salt
75 g (3 oz) butter or
  margarine
1-2 tablespoons iced
  water

First make the pastry and bake blind
in a 20 cm (8 inch) flan tin, as for
Sultana Meringue Pie (see page 86).
  Blend the cornflour with a little of
the pineapple juice in a pan.
  Add the remaining juice and heat
slowly, stirring, until thickened.
Remove from the heat and beat in the
egg yolks and butter. Pour into the
pastry case and cool.
  Whisk the egg whites until very
stiff and dry. Add the sugar a little at
a time, whisking thoroughly between
each addition until the meringue is
glossy and forms soft peaks.
  Spoon into a large piping bag fitted
with a 1 cm (½ inch) star nozzle and
pipe over the pineapple filling.
Sprinkle lightly with a little caster
sugar.
  Bake in a preheated moderate
oven, 160°C (325°F), Gas Mark 3, for
15 to 20 minutes, until golden brown.
  Serve warm or cold, with Vanilla
Cream Sauce.
Serves 6

CHOCOLATE MERINGUES

2 large egg whites
125 g (4 oz) caster
  sugar
50 g (2 oz) plain
  chocolate, grated
170 ml (6 fl oz)
  double cream,
  whipped with
  1 teaspoon caster
  sugar
TO SERVE:
Chocolate Sauce (see
  page 153)

Put the egg whites in a large mixing
bowl and whisk until stiff. Whisk in
2 tablespoons of the sugar. Fold in the
remaining sugar and the grated
chocolate with a metal spoon.
  Spoon the mixture into 16 rounds
on a baking sheet lined with silicone
paper.
  Bake in a very cool oven, 110°C
(225°F), Gas Mark ¼, for about
3 hours or until the meringues are
firm to the touch. Leave on a baking
sheet until completely cold.
  Sandwich the meringues together
with cream. Serve with Chocolate
Sauce handed separately.
Makes 8

APPLE AMBER

500 g (1 lb) cooking
  apples, peeled and
  cored
1 tablespoon water
50 g (2 oz) caster
  sugar
2 egg yolks
grated rind and juice
  of ½ lemon
MERINGUE:
2 egg whites
125 g (4 oz) caster
  sugar
TO SERVE:
Vanilla Cream Sauce
  (see page 153)

Slice the apples into a pan and add the
water and sugar. Cover and cook
gently to a pulp, stirring occasionally,
then beat until smooth. Beat in the
egg yolks, lemon rind and juice and
pour into a 600 ml (1 pint) ovenproof
dish.
  To make the meringue: whisk the
egg whites until stiff. Whisk in
2 tablespoons of the sugar, then fold
in the remainder. Pile on top of the
apple mixture.
  Bake in a preheated moderate
oven, 160°C (325°F), Gas Mark 3, for
20 to 30 minutes until golden. Serve
hot or cold, with Vanilla Cream
Sauce if liked.
Serves 4

PEACH AND RICE MERINGUE

1 × 439 g (15½ oz)
  can creamed rice
  pudding
4 fresh peaches,
  skinned and sliced,
  or 1 × 411 g
  (14½ oz) can
  peach slices,
  drained
4 tablespoons
  redcurrant jelly
juice of ½ lemon
MERINGUE:
2 egg whites
75 g (3 oz) caster
  sugar

Pour the rice into an ovenproof dish and arrange the peach slices on top. Gently warm the redcurrant jelly with the lemon juice, then pour over the peaches.

Whisk the egg whites until stiff, whisk in half the caster sugar, then fold in the rest. Spoon the meringue over the fruit and place in a preheated moderate oven, 180°C (350°F), Gas Mark 4, for 15 to 20 minutes until golden.
Serves 6

Peach and Rice Meringue

SULTANA MERINGUE PIE

SHORTCRUST
  PASTRY:
250 g (8 oz) plain
  flour
pinch of salt
50 g (2 oz) butter
50 g (2 oz) lard
water to mix
FILLING:
175 g (6 oz) sultanas
250 ml (8 fl oz)
  water
75 g (3 oz) brown
  sugar
25 g (1 oz) butter
15 g (½ oz) plain
  flour
2 egg yolks
1 teaspoon grated
  lemon rind
3 tablespoons lemon
  juice
MERINGUE:
2 egg whites
¼ teaspoon cream of
  tartar (optional)
4 tablespoons icing
  sugar, sifted

To make the pastry, sift the flour and salt into a bowl. Rub in the fat until the mixture resembles fine breadcrumbs. Stir in sufficient water to make a fairly stiff dough. Knead lightly, then cover and chill for 30 minutes.

Roll out the dough and use to line a 23 cm (9 inch) flan tin. Line the flan case with greaseproof paper and dried beans. Bake blind in a preheated moderately hot oven, 190°C (375°F), Gas Mark 5, for about 20 minutes or until light golden brown and firm. Remove the beans and paper and allow to cool.

For the filling, put the sultanas and water in a saucepan and bring to the boil. Stir in the brown sugar and remove from the heat. Pour about 4 tablespoons of the mixture into a bowl and mix in the butter and flour. Return this to the saucepan and cook, stirring, until thickened. Remove from the heat and beat in the egg yolks and lemon rind and juice. Pour this filling into the pastry shell.

For the meringue, whisk the egg whites until frothy. Add the cream of tartar if using, and continue whisking until stiff. Gradually beat in the icing sugar.

Spoon the meringue over the filling, spreading it to the pastry rim. Bake in a preheated moderate oven, 180°C (350°F), Gas Mark 4, for 10 to 15 minutes or until the meringue is set and light golden brown.
Serves 6

LEMON MERINGUE PIE

4 tablespoons
   cornflour
300 ml (½ pint)
   water
25 g (1 oz) butter
grated rind and juice
   of 2 small lemons
2 eggs, separated
175 g (6 oz) caster
   sugar
SHORTCRUST
   PASTRY:
175 g (6 oz) plain
   flour
pinch of salt
75 g (3 oz) butter or
   margarine
1-2 tablespoons iced
   water

First make the pastry and bake blind in a 20 cm (8 inch) fluted flan ring, as for Sultana Meringue Pie (see opposite).

Remove the flan ring and cool on a wire rack.

Blend the cornflour with a little of the water in a small pan. Add the remaining water and the butter. Bring to the boil slowly, stirring constantly. Cook, stirring, for 3 minutes. Remove from the heat and add the lemon rind and juice, egg yolks and 50 g (2 oz) of the sugar. Pour into the flan case.

Whisk the egg whites until very stiff, then whisk in 50 g (2 oz) of the sugar. Fold in the remaining sugar and spread over the filling.

Bake in a preheated moderate oven, 160°C (325°F), Gas Mark 3, for 20 to 25 minutes. Serve hot or cold.

Serves 4 to 6

Lemon Cheese Meringue

RUM MERINGUE CAKE

4 egg whites
250 g (8 oz) soft
   light brown sugar
1 teaspoon instant
   coffee powder
FILLING:
125 g (4 oz) plain
   chocolate, melted
   with 3-4
   tablespoons rum
284 ml (10 fl oz)
   double cream,
   lightly whipped

Whisk the egg whites until stiff, then whisk in 1 tablespoon of the brown sugar. Stir the coffee powder into the remaining brown sugar and whisk into the meringue until peaks form.

Spread or pipe into three 18 cm (7 inch) rounds on baking sheets lined with silicone paper. Bake in a preheated cool oven, 140°C (275°F), Gas Mark 1, for 1 to 1½ hours or until crisp. Transfer to a wire rack to cool, then peel off the paper.

Whisk the slightly cooled rum chocolate mixture into the cream.

Sandwich the meringues together with two thirds of the chocolate cream and pipe remainder on top.

Serves 6 to 8

LEMON CHEESE MERINGUE

25 g (1 oz) cornflour
300 ml (½ pint)
   milk
25 g (1 oz)
   granulated sugar
75 g (3 oz) medium-
   fat curd cheese
grated rind and juice
   of 1 lemon
2 eggs, separated
50 g (2 oz) caster
   sugar

Blend the cornflour with a little of the milk, then stir in the granulated sugar. Heat the remaining milk until almost boiling, then pour onto the blended custard, stirring. Return to the heat, stirring, until the custard thickens. Cool slightly.

Blend in the cheese, lemon rind and juice, and egg yolks. Whisk until smooth, then spoon into a greased 600 ml (1 pint) ovenproof dish.

Whisk the egg whites until stiff. Whisk in 25 g (1 oz) of the caster sugar, then fold in the remainder. Pile on top of the lemon custard and bake in a preheated moderately hot oven, 200°C (400°F), Gas Mark 6, for 15 minutes. Serve with cream.

Serves 4

CHOCOLATE HAZELNUT MERINGUE

MERINGUE:
4 egg whites
250 g (8 oz) caster sugar
125 g (4 oz) hazelnuts, toasted and ground

FILLING:
125 g (4 oz) plain chocolate, broken into pieces
4 tablespoons water
426 ml (15 fl oz) double cream

TO FINISH:
50 g (2 oz) chocolate, melted

Whisk the egg whites until stiff then whisk in 2 tablespoons of the sugar. Carefully fold in the remaining sugar a little at a time, with the ground hazelnuts.

Put the meringue into a piping bag fitted with a 1 cm (½ inch) plain nozzle and pipe into two 23 cm (9 inch) rounds on baking sheets lined with silicone paper. Bake in a preheated very cool oven, 120°C (250°F), Gas Mark ½, for 2 hours. Transfer to a wire rack to cool.

Place the chocolate and water in a small pan and heat very gently until melted; cool. Whip the cream until it begins to thicken, then whip in the cooled chocolate and continue to whip until stiff.

Use three-quarters of the chocolate cream to sandwich the meringue rounds together. Pipe the remaining cream around the top edge. Put the melted chocolate in a greaseproof piping bag, snip off the end and drizzle the chocolate across the top of the meringue.
Serves 8

ST VALENTINE'S VACHERIN

MERINGUE BASKET:
4 egg whites
250 g (8 oz) icing sugar, sifted
½ teaspoon vanilla essence

FILLING:
284 ml (10 fl oz) whipping cream, whipped
350 g (12 oz) fresh or frozen raspberries, thawed
3 tablespoons raspberry conserve, sieved and warmed

TOPPING:
icing sugar for sprinkling

Line a baking sheet with silicone paper. Mark a large heart shape on the paper, making it about 20 cm (8 inches) wide and 23 cm (9 inches) long.

Prepare the meringue as for Meringue Cuite (see page 82) and spoon into a large piping bag fitted with a 1 cm (½ inch) star nozzle. Pipe around the outline of the heart then fill in the middle. Pipe large rosettes or swirls around the edge, making a heart-shaped basket.

Place in a very cool oven, 110°C (225°F), Gas Mark ¼, for 4 to 5 hours or until the meringue is completely dry. For a really white meringue, leave in the oven overnight with the door slightly open.

Very carefully lift the meringue basket onto a flat serving dish. Spread the cream over the base, top with raspberries and spoon over the warm conserve.

Sprinkle lightly with icing sugar to serve.
Serves 6

LEMON MERINGUES

4 egg whites
275 g (9 oz) caster sugar
113 g (4 oz) cream cheese
grated rind and juice of 1 lemon
142 ml (5 fl oz) double cream, whipped

TO DECORATE:
6 lemon twists
frosted currant leaves, page 43 (optional)

Whisk the egg whites until stiff, then whisk in half the sugar. Fold in all but 2 tablespoons of the remaining sugar.

Spoon the meringue into 12 mounds on a baking sheet lined with silicone paper. Bake in a preheated cool oven, 140°C (275°F), Gas Mark 1, for 2 hours. Peel off the paper and cool.

Beat together the cheese, reserved sugar, lemon rind and juice. Fold in the cream and use to sandwich the meringues. Decorate with lemon twists and frosted leaves, if desired.
Serves 6

PEACH MERINGUE BASKET

MERINGUE:
5 egg whites
*325 g (11 oz) icing
 sugar, sifted*
*few drops of vanilla
 essence*
FILLING:
*284 ml (10 fl oz)
 double cream,
 lightly whipped*
*6 ripe peaches, peeled
 and sliced*
2 tablespoons kirsch

Whisk the egg whites until stiff, then gradually whisk in the icing sugar with the vanilla. Place the bowl over a pan of simmering water and whisk for about 5 minutes, until very stiff.

Line 2 large baking sheets with silicone paper and draw four 15 cm (6 inch) circles on each. Put most of the meringue in a piping bag fitted with a large fluted nozzle. Pipe a base on one circle and a ring of meringue on the other circles.

Bake in a preheated cool oven, 150°C (300°F), Gas Mark 2, for 50 minutes. Fill the piping bag with the remaining meringue.

Remove the rings from the paper and place one on top of the other on the base, fixing them with a little uncooked meringue. Pipe vertical lines of meringue round the basket. Return to the oven for 1 hour. Cool on a wire rack; remove the paper.

Reserve 2 tablespoons cream. Fold the slices from 4 peaches into the remaining cream, with the kirsch. Spoon into the basket and top with the remaining peach slices and cream.
Serves 6 to 8

FREEZING EGG YOLKS AND WHITES

When making meringues, you are often left with numerous egg yolks to use up; they can, however, be successfully frozen for use at a later date. Add ¼ teaspoon salt or ½ teaspoon sugar to every 3 yolks, depending upon intended use, and pour into rigid containers. Alternatively, place egg yolks individually in ice cube trays, open freeze until solid and then pack in polythene bags, which should be sealed and labelled.

Egg whites may also be frozen in usable quantities or individually in ice cube trays. Both whites and yolks may be frozen for up to six months. To thaw yolks or whites transfer to a bowl and leave for at least 1 hour at room temperature. Use as required, as soon as possible after thawing.

OPPOSITE: *Chocolate Hazelnut Meringue*
RIGHT: *Peach Meringue Basket; Lemon Meringues*

CARAMEL VACHERIN

4 egg whites
250 g (8 oz) soft
    brown sugar
50 g (2 oz)
    hazelnuts,
    browned and
    chopped
284 ml (10 fl oz)
    double cream
8 hazelnuts to
    decorate

Whisk the egg whites on highest speed until stiff and dry looking. Gradually whisk in the sugar. Put the meringue into a piping bag, fitted with a 1 cm (½ inch) plain nozzle. Pipe two 23 cm (9 inch) rounds on baking sheets lined with silicone paper. Sprinkle a few of the chopped nuts over one round.

Bake in a very cool oven, 120°C (250°F), Gas Mark ½, for 2 hours until crisp. Peel off the paper and cool the rounds on a wire rack.

Whip the cream until it holds its shape. Combine three quarters of the cream with the remaining chopped nuts and use to sandwich the meringues together, with the nutty round on top. Pipe the remaining cream around the edge and decorate with the hazelnuts.

Serves 6 to 8

CHESTNUT MERINGUE NESTS

MERINGUE:
3 egg whites
250 g (8 oz) caster
    sugar
FILLING:
½ × 439 g (15½ oz)
    can sweetened
    chestnut purée
1 tablespoon caster
    sugar
2 tablespoons brandy
142 ml (5 fl oz)
    whipping cream,
    whipped
8 chocolate rose
    leaves to decorate
    (see below)

Whisk the egg whites until stiff, then gradually whisk in the caster sugar.

Line a baking sheet with silicone paper and draw eight 7.5 cm (3 inch) circles on the paper. Put the meringue into a piping bag fitted with a large fluted nozzle. Pipe a round to fill each circle; pipe round the edge of each base to form a nest.

Bake in a preheated cool oven, 140°C (275°F), Gas Mark 1, for 1½ hours. Cool on a wire rack. Remove the paper. Beat the chestnut purée with the sugar and brandy until blended, then fold in the cream. Pipe into the nests using a fluted nozzle; decorate each nest with a chocolate rose leaf.

Serves 8

Chocolate rose leaves: Coat the underside of each leaf with melted chocolate, using a fine paint brush. Leave to set, chocolate side up, then carefully lift the tip of the leaf and peel away from the chocolate.

| LEFTOVER EGG YOLKS |

Never discard leftover egg yolks when making meringues as they are essential ingredients of many other dishes. Desserts using egg yolks can be made at the same time as the meringue desserts or the egg yolks can be frozen for use later (see page 89).

The following ice creams incorporate egg yolks in their recipes: Vanilla Ice Cream (see page 31); Orange Ice Cream (see page 32); Blackberry Ice Cream (see page 38); Ginger Ice Cream (see page 45) and Rum and Raisin Ice Cream (see page 45). Other desserts such as Orange Mousse (see page 60); Petits Pots au Chocolat (see page 62); Coffee and Walnut Mousse (see page 69) and Crème Brûlée (see page 70) all incorporate egg yolks. Egg yolks can also be added to many dishes as a thickening agent, for example in Vanilla Cream Sauce (see page 153).

LEFT: *Caramel Vacherin*
OPPOSITE: *Vacherin aux Marrons; Meringue Baskets*

VACHERIN AUX MARRONS

MERINGUE:
5 egg whites
*300 g (10 oz) caster
sugar*
FILLING:
*426 ml (15 fl oz)
double cream*
*227 g (8 oz) can
sweetened chestnut
purée*
2 tablespoons brandy
TO DECORATE:
sifted icing sugar
*25 g (1 oz) grated
chocolate*

Whisk the egg whites until stiff, then whisk in 3 tablespoons of the sugar. Carefully fold in the remaining sugar.

Put the meringue into a piping bag, fitted with a 1 cm (½ inch) plain nozzle. Pipe into three 20 cm (8 inch) rounds on baking sheets lined with silicone paper. Bake in a preheated cool oven, 140°C (275°F), Gas Mark 1, for 1½ to 2 hours. Peel off the paper and cool on a wire rack.

Whip the cream until it holds its shape. Combine three-quarters of the cream with the chestnut purée and brandy. Sandwich the meringue rounds together with this mixture.

Sprinkle with icing sugar and decorate with grated chocolate. Pipe cream around the edge.

Serves 8

MERINGUE BASKETS

MERINGUE:
4 egg whites
*few drops of vanilla
essence*
*275 g (9 oz) icing
sugar, sifted*
FILLING:
*142 ml (5 fl oz)
double cream,
whipped*
*125 g (4 oz)
strawberries*
*2 tablespoons
redcurrant jelly,
warmed*

Whisk the egg whites until stiff, then whisk in the vanilla essence and the icing sugar, a tablespoon at a time. Place the bowl over a pan of gently simmering water and continue whisking for about 5 minutes until the meringue is very stiff.

Line a baking sheet with silicone paper and draw eight 7.5 cm (3 inch) circles on the paper. Spread half the meringue over the circles to form bases. Put the remaining meringue into a piping bag, fitted with a large fluted nozzle, and pipe round the edge of each base.

Bake in a preheated cool oven, 150°C (300°F), Gas Mark 2, for 1 to 1¼ hours. Cool on a wire rack. Remove the paper.

Spoon a little cream into each basket and arrange the strawberries on top. Brush the redcurrant jelly over the strawberries to glaze.

Makes 8

PUDDINGS, PIES AND TRADITIONAL FAVOURITES

Old English puddings have almost become a thing of the past with today's health-conscious trend towards fresh fruit and light desserts. Yet nothing can be more heartening on a bitterly cold winter's day than a steaming hot pudding or crusty fruit pie. These warming dishes are the most appropriate way to round off lighter winter meals.

Here you will find recipes for all those traditional favourites: sustaining steamed puddings like Treacle Pudding (page 106) and Chocolate Sponge Pudding (page 106); baked puddings, such as Apricot Upside-Down Pudding (page 105) and delicious fruit crumbles, including Plum and Walnut Crumble (page 100); batter puddings in the form of crisp pancakes and fritters; not to forget the best known English pudding – Christmas Pudding (page 107).

For pies and crumbles, autumn provides the best selection of fruits – apples, pears, plums and damsons. Use them to make delicious single crust fruit pies, open lattice-topped flans and warming crumbles. Blackberries are another excellent fruit for these desserts – they are especially good combined with apples. Blackberries are available from late July to early September and it is well worth freezing some, if you can, for use in warming winter puddings and pies.

Most of the recipes in this chapter are best served hot with a custard sauce or cream, but don't turn the pages in the summer months! Many of the tarts and fruit flans are delicious served cold with whipped cream – making them ideal for warm days.

BURNT CREAM BANANA PIE

SHORTBREAD
  DOUGH:
*150 g (5 oz) plain
  flour*
75 g (3 oz) butter
*40 g (1½ oz) caster
  sugar*
FILLING:
*1½ tablespoons
  cornflour*
*300 ml (½ pint)
  milk*
*4 tablespoons single
  cream*
4 egg yolks
*15 g (½ oz) caster
  sugar*
*½ teaspoon vanilla
  essence*
1-2 bananas
TOPPING:
*175 g (6 oz) caster or
  demerara sugar*
*banana slices to
  decorate*

Sift the flour into a bowl. Add the butter and sugar and rub in until the mixture resembles breadcrumbs. Press the mixture together into a stiff dough. Knead on a lightly floured surface until smooth.

Place in the centre of a 20 cm (8 inch) flan dish and press with the knuckles until the dough completely covers the base. Prick well and bake on the top shelf of a preheated cool oven, 150°C (300°F), Gas Mark 2, for about 40 minutes, until pale golden and set. Cool in the dish.

Blend the cornflour with the milk in a pan. Bring slowly to the boil, stirring, until thickened. Lower the heat to a minimum. Beat in the cream, egg yolks, sugar and vanilla and heat for 2 to 3 minutes, stirring; do not boil. Cool slightly.

Slice the bananas and arrange over the shortbread base. Cover immediately with the egg custard and chill until set, preferably overnight.

Sprinkle the sugar evenly over the top. Place under a hot grill until the sugar melts and caramelizes. Chill for 2 to 3 hours before serving, decorated with banana slices.
Serves 6 to 8

ROYAL CURD TART

*shortcrust pastry
  made with 250 g
  (8 oz) flour (see
  Treacle Tart, page
  96)*
*227 g (8 oz)
  medium-fat curd
  cheese*
*50 g (2 oz) ground
  almonds*
*50 g (2 oz) caster
  sugar*
*2 eggs, separated
grated rind and juice
  of 1 lemon*
50 g (2 oz) sultanas
*142 ml (5 fl oz)
  double cream*
icing sugar to decorate

Roll out the pastry and use to line a 23 cm (9 inch) flan ring placed on a baking sheet. Prick the base.

Place the cheese in a bowl and blend in the ground almonds, caster sugar and egg yolks. Add the lemon rind and juice, sultanas and cream and mix well. Whisk the egg whites until stiff and fold into the mixture. Pour into the flan case and bake in a preheated moderately hot oven, 200°C (400°F), Gas Mark 6, for 20 minutes. Lower the temperature to 180°C (350°F), Gas Mark 4, and continue to cook for 30 to 35 minutes until firm and golden.

Serve warm or chilled, dusted with icing sugar.
Serves 6

BAKED CUSTARD TART

*1 quantity shortcrust
  pastry (see Pecan
  Pie, opposite)*
4 eggs
*25 g (1 oz) caster
  sugar*
*½ teaspoon vanilla
  essence*
*450 ml (¾ pint)
  milk*
grated nutmeg

Prepare and cook a 20 cm (8 inch) flan case as for Pecan Pie.

Lightly whisk the eggs with the sugar and vanilla essence in a bowl. Heat the milk until warm and whisk in the eggs. Strain into the flan case and sprinkle with nutmeg.

Bake in a preheated moderate oven, 160°C (325°F), Gas Mark 3, for 45 to 50 minutes, until set and lightly browned. Serve warm or cold.
Serves 6

PECAN PIE

**SHORTCRUST
PASTRY:**
*175 g (6 oz) plain
flour*
125 g (4 oz) butter
1 egg yolk
*2-3 teaspoons cold
water*
FILLING:
25 g (1 oz) butter
*125 g (4 oz) caster
sugar*
*175 g (6 oz) maple
or golden syrup*
4 eggs (size 1 or 2)
*1 teaspoon vanilla
essence*
*50 g (2 oz) pecan
nuts or walnuts,
chopped*

Sift the flour into a mixing bowl. Rub in the butter until the mixture resembles breadcrumbs. Add the egg yolk and water and mix to a firm dough. Knead lightly on a floured surface until smooth. Roll out and use to line a 20 cm (8 inch) fluted flan ring or pie dish. If possible, chill for 20 to 30 minutes.

Line with greaseproof paper and dried beans and bake blind on the top shelf of a preheated moderately hot oven, 200°C (400°F), Gas Mark 6, for 15 to 20 minutes. Remove the beans and paper and return to the oven for 5 minutes. Cool and remove the flan ring, if used.

Cream the butter and sugar until very soft and creamy. Gradually beat in the syrup, then beat in the eggs, one at a time, and vanilla essence (the mixture may curdle). Pour into the pastry case and sprinkle over the nuts.

Bake in a preheated hot oven, 220°C (425°F), Gas Mark 7, for 10 minutes, then lower the temperature to 180°C (350°F), Gas Mark 4, and cook for 30 to 35 minutes. Serve cool, with whipped cream if desired.
Serves 6 to 8

TIPS ON MAKING SHORTCRUST PASTRY

One of the most important features of making good shortcrust pastry is that all the ingredients and equipment should be kept as cool as possible. When rubbing in, kneading and rolling out, pastry should be handled very lightly. If you have time, chill the pastry before using.

Choice of fat for pastry-making depends upon personal preference. The best compromise is often to use half quantities of lard and margarine, or half a quantity of lard, a quarter margarine and a quarter butter. Leftover pastry and both baked and unbaked dishes freeze well. Ready-baked dishes, such as fruit pies, can be cooked successfully from frozen, by allowing a little extra cooking time.

OPPOSITE: *Royal Curd Tart*
RIGHT: *Pecan Pie; Baked Custard Tart*

TREACLE TART

**SHORTCRUST
PASTRY:**
175 g (6 oz) plain
flour
75 g (3 oz) butter or
margarine
1-2 tablespoons iced
water
FILLING:
250 g (8 oz) golden
syrup
75 g (3 oz) fresh
white breadcrumbs
grated rind of
½ lemon

Sift the flour into a bowl. Rub in the butter or margarine until the mixture resembles fine breadcrumbs. Add the water gradually and mix to a firm dough.

Turn out onto a floured surface and knead lightly. Roll out thinly to a 23 cm (9 inch) circle. Use to line an 18 cm (7 inch) flan ring placed on a baking sheet. Chill the flan and pastry trimmings for 15 minutes.

Mix the syrup, breadcrumbs and lemon rind together and spread over the pastry. Roll out the trimmings, cut into long narrow strips and make a lattice pattern over the filling.

Bake in a preheated moderately hot oven, 200°C (400°F), Gas Mark 6, for 30 minutes. Serve warm with cream.
Serves 4 to 6

SPICED APPLE PIE

750 g (1½ lb)
cooking apples,
peeled, cored and
thinly sliced
75 g (3 oz) soft
brown sugar
½ teaspoon ground
cinnamon
½ teaspoon grated
nutmeg
4 cloves
1 quantity shortcrust
pastry (see Treacle
Tart, right)
water and caster sugar
to glaze
**CRÈME À LA
VANILLE:**
2 egg yolks
1 teaspoon cornflour
25 g (1 oz) caster
sugar
300 ml (½ pint)
milk
½ teaspoon vanilla
essence

Layer the apples with the sugar and spices in a 900 ml (1½ pint) pie dish, finishing with a layer of apples.

Roll out the pastry thinly to a circle about 5 cm (2 inches) larger than the pie dish. Cut off a narrow strip all round and use to cover the dampened rim of the pie dish; brush with water.

Lift the pastry onto the rolling pin and place over the apples, sealing the edges well. Trim and flute the edges; make a hole in the centre.

Brush with water, sprinkle with sugar and bake in a preheated hot oven, 200°C (400°F), Gas Mark 6, for 30 to 40 minutes.

To make crème à la vanille: cream the egg yolks with the cornflour and sugar. Bring the milk to the boil, pour onto the egg yolk mixture and stir well.

Return to the pan and heat gently, stirring constantly, until the mixture is thick enough to coat the back of a spoon. Add the essence then strain.

Serve the pie hot or cold with the crème à la vanille handed separately.
Serves 4 to 6

STRAWBERRY TARTS

PÂTE SUCRÉE:
125 g (4 oz) plain
flour
50 g (2 oz) butter,
softened
50 g (2 oz) caster
sugar
2 egg yolks
few drops of vanilla
essence
GLAZE:
4 tablespoons
redcurrant jelly
1 tablespoon water
FILLING:
250 g (8 oz)
strawberries

Sift the flour onto a board, make a well in the centre and place the butter, sugar, egg yolks and vanilla in the well. Using the fingertips of one hand, work these ingredients together until well blended, then draw in the flour. Knead lightly until smooth and chill for 1 hour.

Roll out the pastry very thinly and use to line 14 patty tins, then press a piece of foil into each. Bake blind in a preheated moderately hot oven, 190°C (375°F), Gas Mark 5, for 10 minutes or until golden. Cool, then remove foil and turn out.

For the glaze, heat the redcurrant jelly with the water. Bring to the boil, sieve and reheat. Brush the cases with glaze. Arrange the fruit in the cases and brush with the remaining glaze.
Makes 14

LEFT: *Spiced Apple Pie*
OPPOSITE: *Franzipan Flan; Cherry and Almond Tart*

FRANZIPAN FLAN

1 quantity rich short-
  crust pastry (see
  Mince Pies, page 98)
50 g (2 oz) cake
  crumbs
1 × 411 g (14½ oz)
  can red cherries,
  drained and stoned
50 g (2 oz) butter
50 g (2 oz) caster
  sugar
1 egg
25 g (1 oz) plain
  flour
75 g (3 oz) ground
  almonds
1 teaspoon rosewater
  (optional)
1 tablespoon icing
  sugar, sifted

Roll out the pastry on a floured surface and use to line a 20 cm (8 inch) flan ring or tin. Bake blind in a preheated moderately hot oven, 200°C (400°F), Gas Mark 6 for 10 minutes. Lower the temperature to 180°C (350°F), Gas Mark 4.

Sprinkle the cake crumbs over the base and arrange the cherries on top.

Place the butter and sugar in a mixing bowl and beat until light and fluffy. Beat in the egg, flour, ground almonds and rosewater, if using. Spread over the cherries and return to the oven for 30 to 40 minutes, until firm to the touch.

Sprinkle with the icing sugar and serve warm or cold.

Serves 6

CHERRY AND ALMOND TART

1 quantity rich
  shortcrust pastry
  (see Mince Pies,
  page 98)
50 g (2 oz) ground
  almonds
4-6 drops of almond
  essence
1 quantity Crème
  Patissière (see page
  138)
500 g (1 lb) dessert
  cherries, halved
  and stoned
175 g (6 oz)
  redcurrant jelly
2 tablespoons water

Roll out the pastry on a floured surface and use to line a 20 cm (8 inch) flan tin or dish. Bake blind in a preheated moderately hot oven, 200°C (400°F), Gas Mark 6, for 20 minutes.

Stir the ground almonds and almond essence into the crème patissière and spread over the base of the flan. Arrange the cherries on top.

Place the redcurrant jelly and water in a small pan and heat gently, stirring, until the jelly dissolves. Brush over the cherries. Serve cold.

Serves 6

NOTE: Any fresh fruit in season, canned or frozen fruit, can be used instead of cherries. Fresh strawberries, raspberries and peach slices are particularly successful.

MINCE PIES

RICH SHORTCRUST
    PASTRY:
*250 g (8 oz) plain
    flour*
150 g (5 oz) butter
*1 tablespoon caster
    sugar*
1 egg yolk
*1-2 tablespoons cold
    water*
milk to glaze
FILLING:
*4-5 tablespoons
    mincemeat*
1 tablespoon brandy
TO SERVE:
sifted icing sugar

Sift the flour into a bowl and rub in the butter until the mixture resembles breadcrumbs. Stir in the sugar. Add the egg yolk and enough water to mix to a firm dough. Knead the dough lightly and chill for 15 minutes.

Roll out half the pastry fairly thinly on a floured surface and cut out 10 to 12 rounds, using a 6 cm (2½ inch) fluted cutter. Roll out the other half of the pastry a little thinner than the first, cut out 7.5 cm (3 inch) rounds and use to line 10 to 12 patty tins.

Mix the mincemeat with the brandy and divide between the patty tins. Dampen the edges of the pastry, place the smaller rounds on top and press the edges together. Make a hole in the centre of each and brush with milk.

Bake in a preheated moderately hot oven, 200°C (400°F), Gas Mark 6, for 15 to 20 minutes until golden. Sprinkle with icing sugar and serve warm.
Makes 10 to 12

PLUM FLAN

SWEET PASTRY:
*175 g (6 oz) plain
    flour*
*40 g (1½ oz)
    margarine*
*25 g (1 oz) caster
    sugar*
40 g (1½ oz) lard
1-2 tablespoons water
FILLING:
*1 tablespoon digestive
    biscuit crumbs*
*500 g (1 lb) dessert
    plums, halved and
    stoned*
*50 g (2 oz) soft
    brown sugar*
*½ teaspoon ground
    cinnamon*

Sift the flour into a bowl and rub in the fat until the mixture resembles breadcrumbs. Stir in the sugar and enough water to make a firm dough. Knead lightly until smooth.

Roll out and use to line a 20 cm (8 inch) flan tin. Bake blind in a preheated moderately hot oven, 200°C (400°F), Gas Mark 6, for 10 minutes.

Sprinkle the biscuit crumbs in the cooked pastry case and arrange the plum halves on top, skin side upwards, overlapping if necessary.

Mix together the sugar, cinnamon and flaked almonds, if using, and sprinkle over the plums.

Bake in a hot oven, 220°C (425°F), Gas Mark 7, for 40 minutes. Serve hot or cold, with cream.
Serves 6 to 8

BLACKCURRANT FLAN

PASTRY:
*175 g (6 oz) plain
    flour*
*2 teaspoons ground
    cinnamon*
125 g (4 oz) butter
*25 g (1 oz) caster
    sugar*
1 egg yolk
2 teaspoons water
*water and caster sugar
    to glaze*
FILLING:
*500 g (1 lb)
    blackcurrants*
*125 g (4 oz)
    demerara sugar*

Sift the flour and cinnamon into a bowl. Rub in the butter until the mixture resembles breadcrumbs. Stir in the caster sugar. Add the egg yolk and water and mix to a firm dough.

Knead lightly, then roll out thinly on a floured surface and use to line an 18 cm (7 inch) flan ring. Chill the flan and trimmings for 15 minutes.

Put the blackcurrants and demerara sugar in a pan. Cover and cook gently for 10 minutes, then uncover and cook quickly until syrupy. Turn onto a plate to cool.

Place the fruit in the flan case. Roll out the pastry trimmings, cut into strips and make a lattice pattern over the fruit. Brush with water and sprinkle with caster sugar.

Bake in a preheated moderately hot oven, 200°C (400°F), Gas Mark 6, for 25 to 30 minutes, until golden.

Serve warm or cold, with cream.
Serves 4 to 6

APPLE AND ORANGE FLAN

1 quantity sweet
    pastry (see plum
    flan, opposite)
1 kg (2 lb) cooking
    apples, peeled and
    cored
1 tablespoon water
50 g (2 oz) caster
    sugar
3 oranges
GLAZE:
4 tablespoons apricot
    jam
2 tablespoons water
1 teaspoon lemon
    juice
TO SERVE:
whipped cream

Roll out the pastry and use to line a
20 cm (8 inch) flan ring standing on a
baking sheet. Line with greaseproof
paper and dried beans and bake in a
preheated moderately hot oven,
200°C (400°F), Gas Mark 6, for 15 to
20 minutes. Remove the paper and
beans and return to the oven for 5
minutes. Remove the flan ring and
cool on a wire rack.

Slice the apples and place in a pan
with the water and sugar. Cover and
cook gently to a pulp, stirring
occasionally. Cool slightly, then
place in a blender or food processor
and work to a purée. Return to the
pan and add the grated rind of
2 oranges. Cook, uncovered, until
thick, stirring occasionally. Leave
until cool, then turn into the flan case
and smooth evenly.

Peel the oranges, removing all pith.
Slice thinly and arrange on top of the
flan. Heat the jam with the water and
lemon juice, then sieve and reheat.
Brush over the oranges. Serve with
whipped cream.
Serves 6

MINCEMEAT FLAN

1 quantity rich
    shortcrust pastry
    (see Mince Pies,
    opposite)
water and caster sugar
    to glaze
FILLING:
500 g (1 lb)
    mincemeat
2 dessert apples,
    peeled, cored and
    chopped
125 g (4 oz) grapes,
    halved and seeded
grated rind of
    1 orange
2 tablespoons brandy
TO SERVE:
1 tablespoon brandy
142 ml (5 fl oz)
    double cream,
    whipped

Roll out two-thirds of the pastry
thinly on a floured surface and use to
line a 23 cm (9 inch) fluted flan ring.
Chill the flan and remaining pastry
for 15 minutes.

Mix the filling ingredients together
and use to fill the flan case.

Roll out the remaining pastry
thinly and cut out about twelve
7.5 cm (3 inch) rounds, with a fluted
cutter. Dampen the edges of the
pastry in the flan ring and arrange the
rounds overlapping around the edge.

Brush with water, sprinkle with
caster sugar and bake in a preheated
moderately hot oven, 200°C (400°F),
Gas Mark 6, for 35 to 40 minutes
until golden.

Fold the brandy into the cream.
Serve the flan hot or cold, topped
with the brandy cream.
Serves 6 to 8

TO MAKE MINCEMEAT

Making mincemeat is a very simple yet rewarding task as the
results are delicious. Peel and core 1 kg (2 lb) apples. Grate
the apples, with 350 g (12 oz) carrots, into a large bowl. Add
250 g (8 oz) cut mixed peel; 750 g (1½ lb) each of currants,
sultanas and sugar; 350 g (12 oz) shredded suet; 50 g (2 oz)
blanched almonds, chopped; 1½ teaspoons ground mixed
spice and 1 teaspoon grated nutmeg. Mix the ingredients
well together. Cover and leave for 24 hours, then add 150 ml
(¼ pint) brandy or rum and mix again. Pack into sterilized
jars and cover.

If the mincemeat is to be kept for more than a few weeks,
seal with airtight covers such as glass or plastic-coated lids.
This quantity of ingredients will make about 4 kg (9 lb)
mincemeat.

OPPOSITE: *Mince Pies*
RIGHT: *Mincemeat Flan*

18th CENTURY TART

½ quantity rich shortcrust pastry (see Mince Pies, page 98)
75 g (3 oz) butter
75 g (3 oz) caster sugar
4 egg yolks
25 g (1 oz) candied peel
grated rind of 1 orange
1 dessert apple

Roll out the pastry on a floured surface and use to line an 18 cm (7 inch) flan ring or tin.

Place the butter, sugar and egg yolks in a mixing bowl and beat with a rotary whisk until light and fluffy. Stir in the candied peel and orange rind. Smooth over the pastry.

Quarter, core and grate the apple (do not peel) and spoon over the flan. Bake in a preheated moderate oven, 180°C (350°F), Gas Mark 4, for 30 minutes. Serve warm or cold.
Serves 4

GERMAN APPLE PUDDING

125 g (4 oz) self-raising flour
25 g (1 oz) ground almonds
75 g (3 oz) butter
50 g (2 oz) soft brown sugar
1 teaspoon lemon juice
1 egg yolk
FILLING:
500 g (1 lb) cooking apples, peeled and cored
75 g (3 oz) soft brown sugar
grated rind of 1 lemon
1 teaspoon lemon juice
TOPPING:
50 g (2 oz) plain flour
50 g (2 oz) butter
150 g (5 oz) soft brown sugar
1 teaspoon ground cinnamon

Place the flour and ground almonds in a mixing bowl and rub in the butter until it resembles fine breadcrumbs.

Stir in the sugar, then mix in the lemon juice and egg yolk. Press into a greased 20 cm (8 inch) loose-bottomed cake tin.

Slice the apples finely and mix with the remaining filling ingredients. Arrange over the sponge mixture.

Sift the flour into a mixing bowl. Rub in the butter until evenly combined. Stir in the sugar and cinnamon. Sprinkle on top of the apples.

Bake in a preheated moderate oven, 180°C (350°F), Gas Mark 4, for 1 to 1¼ hours, until golden. Cool slightly, then carefully push out of the tin and slide onto a serving plate. Serve hot or cold.
Serves 4

BLACKBERRY AND APPLE CRUMBLE

75 g (3 oz) butter
175 g (6 oz) wholewheat flour
75 g (3 oz) demerara sugar
500 g (1 lb) cooking apples, peeled, cored and sliced
250 g (8 oz) blackberries
75 g (3 oz) sugar

Rub the butter into the flour until the mixture resembles breadcrumbs, then stir in the demerara sugar.

Layer the apples, blackberries and sugar in a 900 ml (1½ pint) ovenproof dish.

Sprinkle the crumble mixture over the fruit to cover completely. Bake in a preheated moderate oven, 180°C (350°F), Gas Mark 4, for 40 to 50 minutes until golden brown.

Serve hot or cold with Crème à la Vanille (see Spiced Apple Pie, page 96).
Serves 4 to 6
VARIATION: For Blackberry and Pear Crumble substitute 500 g (1 lb) cooking pears for the cooking apples. Make as above; however, bake in a preheated moderately hot oven, 200°C (400°F), Gas Mark 6, for 15 minutes, then reduce the temperature to 190°C (375°F), Gas Mark 5, and bake for a further 20 to 25 minutes.

PLUM AND WALNUT CRUMBLE

500 g (1 lb) plums, halved and stoned
75 g (3 oz) granulated sugar
175 g (6 oz) plain flour
75 g (3 oz) butter
75 g (3 oz) demerara sugar
125 g (4 oz) walnut pieces

Arrange the plums in a 1.2 litre (2 pint) ovenproof dish and sprinkle with the granulated sugar.

Sift the flour into a mixing bowl. Rub in the butter until it resembles fine breadcrumbs. Stir in the sugar and walnut pieces.

Spoon the crumble over the fruit. Bake in a preheated moderate oven, 180°C (350°F), Gas Mark 4, for 30 to 40 minutes, until golden. Serve hot.
Serves 4
NOTE: Try other combinations: cherry and almond, apple and mixed nuts.

Plum and Walnut Crumble; 18th Century Tart; German Apple Pudding

CHOCOLATE FUDGE PUDDING

FUDGE TOPPING:
40 g (1½ oz) butter
40 g (1½ oz) soft dark brown sugar
40 g (1½ oz) golden syrup
15 g (½ oz) cocoa powder
2 tablespoons single or half cream
50 g (2 oz) walnuts or pecans, finely chopped

CAKE MIXTURE:
2 eggs
125 g (4 oz) caster sugar
125 g (4 oz) butter or margarine
125 g (4 oz) self-raising flour
1 teaspoon baking powder

Place all the fudge ingredients in a small heavy-based pan. Heat gently until boiling, stirring constantly, and boil for 30 seconds. Pour into a lined and greased 20 cm (8 inch) sandwich tin, or a well greased 1.5 litre (2½ pint) ring mould. Leave until cold.

Place the cake mixture ingredients in a large mixing bowl and beat with a wooden spoon for 2 minutes. Turn onto the cooled fudge mixture and spread evenly with a palette knife.

Bake in a preheated moderate oven, 160°C (325°F), Gas Mark 3, for 40 to 45 minutes, until well risen, golden brown and firm to the touch. Leave in the tin for 5 minutes.

Invert onto a serving plate and peel off the lining paper. The fudge mixture forms a soft, sticky topping which will run down the sides.

Serve hot with cream or Vanilla Cream Sauce (see page 153).
Serves 6 to 8

GINGER QUEEN OF PUDDINGS

600 ml (1 pint) milk
pared rind of ½ lemon
50 g (2 oz) butter
175 g (6 oz) caster sugar
75 g (3 oz) fine fresh white breadcrumbs
3 eggs, separated
3-4 tablespoons ginger marmalade

Put the milk and lemon rind in a pan over a very low heat and leave for 10 minutes. Discard the lemon rind.

Add the butter and 50 g (2 oz) of the sugar to the milk and stir until melted. Add the breadcrumbs and egg yolks and mix well. Transfer to a well-buttered shallow 1.2 litre (2 pint) ovenproof dish.

Leave to stand for 10 minutes then bake in a preheated moderate oven, 180°C (350°F), Gas Mark 4, for 15 to 20 minutes or until set. Cool slightly, then spread with the marmalade.

Whisk the egg whites until stiff. Whisk in half the remaining sugar, then fold in all but 2 teaspoons of the rest. Pipe or spoon the meringue over the baked pudding and sprinkle with the reserved sugar. Return to a cool oven, 150°C (300°F), Gas Mark 2, for 8 to 10 minutes, until golden brown.

Serve warm.
Serves 6

APPLE MERINGUE

750 g (1½ lb)
  cooking apples,
  peeled, cored and
  sliced
50 g (2 oz)
  granulated sugar
  (approximately)
1 jam Swiss roll,
  sliced
grated rind and juice
  of 1 lemon
2 egg whites
125 g (4 oz) caster
  sugar

Put the apples in a saucepan with a little water and granulated sugar to taste. Bring to the boil and simmer for about 15 minutes or until soft. Work to a smooth purée in an electric blender, or beat with a spoon and then rub through a sieve.

Line the base of a 1.75 litre (3 pint) soufflé dish with the Swiss roll. Spoon over the lemon rind and juice. Spread the apple purée over the top.

Whisk the egg whites until stiff. Whisk in half the caster sugar, then fold in the remainder.

Pile the meringue over the apple. Bake in a preheated cool oven, 150°C (300°F), Gas Mark 2, for 30 minutes until the meringue is golden. Serve hot.

Serves 4 to 6

BLACKBERRY AND APPLE LAYER

125 g (4 oz) butter
500 g (1 lb) cooking
  apples, peeled,
  cored and sliced
250 g (8 oz)
  blackberries
75 g (3 oz) demerara
  sugar
125 g (4 oz) fresh
  breadcrumbs

Melt 25 g (1 oz) of the butter in a pan. Add the apples, blackberries and 25 g (1 oz) of the sugar. Cover and simmer gently until soft but not pulpy.

Melt the remaining butter in a frying pan and fry the breadcrumbs until golden brown. Cool, then add the remaining sugar.

Divide half the fruit between 4 individual glass dishes and cover with half the crumbs, then repeat the layers.

Serve chilled with whipped cream.
Serves 4

QUEEN PUDDING

75 g (3 oz) white
  bread, crusts
  removed
450 ml (¾ pint)
  milk
40 g (1½ oz) butter
2 eggs, separated
75 g (3 oz) caster
  sugar
grated rind of 1 lemon
3 tablespoons jam

Cut the bread into small cubes or grate coarsely and place in a greased 1.2 litre (2 pint) ovenproof dish.

Heat the milk and butter until just warm. Beat the egg yolks with half the sugar. Add the lemon rind and pour on the warmed milk, stirring well. Pour this custard over the bread and bake in a preheated moderate oven, 180°C (350°F), Gas Mark 4, for 25 minutes or until set.

Warm the jam and spread it over the pudding. Whisk the egg whites until stiff and fold in the remaining sugar. Pile the meringue on top of the jam and return to the oven for a further 10 to 15 minutes until the meringue is crisp.

Serves 4

OPPOSITE: *Chocolate Fudge Pudding; Ginger Queen of Puddings*
RIGHT: *Queen Pudding*

PINEAPPLE PUDDING

1 × 439 g (15½ oz) can pineapple slices, drained
15 g (½ oz) angelica
125 g (4 oz) butter or margarine
125 g (4 oz) caster sugar
grated rind and juice of 1 lemon
2 eggs
150 g (5 oz) self-raising flour, sifted

Butter a 900 ml (1½ pint) pudding basin and arrange the pineapple slices around the base and sides. Place a piece of angelica in the centre of each.

Cream the butter or margarine, sugar and lemon rind together until light and fluffy. Add the eggs, one at a time, adding a little flour with the second egg. Beat thoroughly, then fold in the remaining flour with the lemon juice.

Turn the mixture into the basin. Cover with buttered foil, making a pleat across the centre to allow the pudding to rise. Steam for 1½ to 2 hours.

Turn out onto a warmed serving dish. Serve with Crème à la Vanille (see Spiced Apple Pie, page 96).

Serves 4

GINGER GOOSEBERRY PUDDING

2 × 283 g (10 oz) cans gooseberries
2 teaspoons ground ginger
75 g (3 oz) soft margarine
75 g (3 oz) caster sugar
1 egg, beaten
125 g (4 oz) self-raising flour
1-2 tablespoons milk

Drain the gooseberries, reserving the syrup. Place the gooseberries in a greased ovenproof dish, pour 2 tablespoons of the syrup over them and sprinkle with half the ginger.

Place the margarine, sugar, egg, flour, milk and remaining ginger in a bowl and beat for 2 to 3 minutes until smooth. Spoon over the fruit.

Bake in a preheated moderate oven, 180°C (350°F), Gas Mark 4, for 40 to 45 minutes.

Warm the remaining syrup and serve with the pudding.

Serves 4

LEMON PUDDING

50 g (2 oz) butter or margarine
grated rind and juice of 1 large lemon
75 g (3 oz) caster sugar
2 eggs, separated
25 g (1 oz) plain flour, sifted
175 ml (6 fl oz) milk

Cream the butter or margarine with the lemon rind and sugar until light and fluffy. Mix in the egg yolks, flour and lemon juice, then gradually stir in the milk. Whisk egg whites until stiff; fold into the mixture.

Turn into a greased 600 ml (1 pint) ovenproof dish and place in a roasting pan, containing 2.5 cm (1 inch) water. Bake in a preheated moderate oven, 180°C (350°F), Gas Mark 4, for 40 to 45 minutes. Serve hot.

Serves 4

Pineapple Pudding

TO PRESSURE COOK STEAMED PUDDINGS

Steamed puddings, which have a steaming time of 1½ to 2 hours can be cooked in the pressure cooker as follows: cover the pudding with a sheet of foil, making a pleat across the centre. Secure with string. Stand the basin on the trivet in the pressure cooker and pour in 750 ml (1½ pints) boiling water. Put the lid on and steam for 25 minutes. Put the weight on, heat to high pressure and cook for 25 minutes. Serve as instructed in given recipe.

CHOCOLATE AND PINEAPPLE UPSIDE-DOWN PUDDING

1 × 227 g (8 oz) can pineapple slices
2-3 tablespoons golden syrup
125 g (4 oz) butter or margarine
125 g (4 oz) caster sugar
2 eggs, beaten
125 g (4 oz) self-raising flour
25 g (1 oz) cocoa

Drain the pineapple slices, reserving the syrup. Pour the golden syrup into a greased 18 cm (7 inch) round cake tin and arrange the pineapple slices on top.

Cream together the fat and sugar until fluffy, then beat in the eggs a little at a time. Sift the flour and cocoa together, then fold into the mixture, adding about 1 tablespoon of the reserved pineapple syrup, to give a smooth dropping consistency.

Spread the mixture over the pineapple and bake in a preheated moderate oven, 180°C (350°F), Gas Mark 4, for about 45 minutes.

Invert onto a plate. Warm the reserved syrup and serve separately.
Serves 4 to 6

APRICOT UPSIDE-DOWN PUDDING

175 g (6 oz) butter or margarine
50 g (2 oz) soft brown sugar
1 × 411 g (14½ oz) can apricot halves, or 6 cooked fresh apricots, halved and stoned
125 g (4 oz) caster sugar
2 eggs
125 g (4 oz) self-raising flour, sifted
1 teaspoon ground mixed spice

Cream 50 g (2 oz) of the fat, mix with the brown sugar and spread over the bottom of a 1.2 litre (2 pint) ovenproof dish. Drain the apricots, reserving 1 tablespoon juice. Arrange in the dish.

Cream the remaining fat with the caster sugar until light and fluffy. Add the eggs, one at a time, adding a tablespoon of the flour with the last one. Beat thoroughly, then fold in the remaining flour, mixed spice and reserved apricot juice.

Spread over the apricots and bake in a preheated moderate oven, 180°C (350°F), Gas Mark 4, for about 45 minutes, or until the sponge springs back when lightly pressed.

Serve with Crème à la Vanille (see Spiced Apple Pie, page 96).
Serves 6

Eve's Pudding

EVE'S PUDDING

500 g (1 lb) cooking apples, peeled, cored and thinly sliced
50 g (2 oz) soft brown sugar
125 g (4 oz) butter or margarine
125 g (4 oz) caster sugar
2 eggs
125 g (4 oz) self-raising flour, sifted
1 tablespoon hot water

Put the apples in a greased 1.2 litre (2 pint) shallow ovenproof dish and sprinkle with the brown sugar.

Cream the butter or margarine with the caster sugar until light and fluffy. Add the eggs, one at a time, adding a little flour with the second egg. Fold in the remaining flour, then the hot water.

Spread the mixture evenly over the apples and bake in a preheated moderate oven, 180°C (350°F), Gas Mark 4, for 40 to 45 minutes until golden brown.

Serve with cream or custard.
Serves 4

TREACLE PUDDING

*125 g (4 oz) butter
   or margarine*
*125 g (4 oz) caster
   sugar*
2 size 1 eggs
*125 g (4 oz)
   self-raising flour,
   sifted*
*4 tablespoons golden
   syrup*
SAUCE:
*4 tablespoons golden
   syrup*
1 tablespoon water

Cream the butter or margarine and sugar together until light and fluffy. Beat in the eggs, one at a time, adding a little of the flour with the second egg. Fold in the remaining flour.

Butter a 900 ml (1½ pint) pudding basin and spoon in the syrup, then put the sponge mixture on top. Cover with buttered foil, making a pleat across the centre to allow the pudding to rise. Steam for 1½ to 2 hours.

To make the sauce: heat the syrup and water in a small pan. Turn the pudding out onto a warmed serving dish and pour the hot sauce over before serving.
Serves 4

CHOCOLATE PUDDING

SPONGE MIXTURE:
*175 g (6 oz) self-
   raising flour*
*2 tablespoons cocoa
   powder*
*125 g (4 oz) butter or
   margarine*
*125 g (4 oz) caster
   sugar*
2 size 1 eggs
2 tablespoons milk
CHOCOLATE SAUCE:
*75 g (3 oz) plain
   chocolate, broken
   into pieces*
*3 tablespoons golden
   syrup*
2 tablespoons water

Sift the flour and cocoa together. Cream the fat and sugar together until light and fluffy. Beat in the eggs, one at a time, adding a little of the flour and cocoa with the second egg. Fold in the remaining flour and cocoa, then mix in the milk.

Spoon the mixture into a buttered 1.2 litre (2 pint) pudding basin. Cover with buttered foil, making a pleat across the centre to allow the pudding to rise. Steam for 1½ to 2 hours.

To make the sauce: melt the chocolate with the syrup and water in a small bowl over a pan of boiling water, then beat until smooth.

Turn the pudding out onto a warmed serving dish and pour the hot sauce over before serving.
Serves 4

CHRISTMAS PUDDING

175 g (6 oz) plain flour
2 teaspoons ground mixed spice
1 teaspoon ground cinnamon
½ teaspoon grated nutmeg
175 g (6 oz) fresh white breadcrumbs
175 g (6 oz) butter
175 g (6 oz) soft brown sugar
350 g (12 oz) sultanas
250 g (8 oz) raisins
250 g (8 oz) currants
75 g (3 oz) chopped mixed peel
grated rind and juice of 1 orange
2 eggs, beaten
120 ml (4 fl oz) brown ale

Sift the flour and spices into a bowl, add the breadcrumbs, then rub in the butter. Stir in the sugar, add the remaining ingredients and mix thoroughly.

Turn into a greased 1.75 litre (3 pint) pudding basin, cover with a pudding cloth or greaseproof paper and foil, and steam for 6 hours, topping up the pan with boiling water as necessary.

Cool slightly, then remove the cloth or paper and leave to cool completely. Cover with clean greaseproof paper and foil and store in a cool dry place.

To serve, steam the pudding again for 2 to 2½ hours. Turn out onto a warmed serving dish. If liked, pour over 2 to 3 tablespoons warmed brandy and ignite. Top with a sprig of holly and serve with cream or Brandy Butter.

Serves 8 to 10

NOTE: Christmas Pudding improves with keeping as it allows the mixture to mature. If possible, make it 3 to 4 months before Christmas.

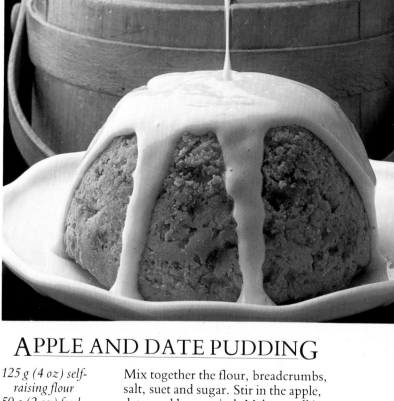

HONEY AND LEMON SPONGE

3 tablespoons clear honey
125 g (4 oz) self-raising flour
1 teaspoon baking powder
125 g (4 oz) soft margarine
125 g (4 oz) caster sugar
2 eggs
grated rind and juice of 1 lemon

Spoon the honey into a buttered 1.2 litre (2 pint) pudding basin.

Sift the flour and baking powder into a bowl, add the remaining ingredients and beat with an electric mixer for 1 minute.

Turn the mixture into the basin and smooth the top. Cover with buttered foil, making a pleat across the centre. Steam for 1½ to 2 hours.

Turn the pudding out onto a warmed serving dish and serve with cream.

Serves 4 to 6

OPPOSITE: *Treacle Pudding; Chocolate Sponge Pudding*
RIGHT: *Apple and Date Pudding*

APPLE AND DATE PUDDING

125 g (4 oz) self-raising flour
50 g (2 oz) fresh white breadcrumbs
pinch of salt
75 g (3 oz) shredded suet
25 g (1 oz) caster sugar
125 g (4 oz) apple, peeled and finely chopped
125 g (4 oz) dates, chopped
grated rind of 1 lemon
150 ml (¼ pint) milk (approximately)

Mix together the flour, breadcrumbs, salt, suet and sugar. Stir in the apple, dates and lemon rind. Make a well in the centre and add enough milk to give a soft dropping consistency. Transfer to a greased 900 ml (1½ pint) pudding basin, cover with greased foil, pleated down the centre, and tie up with string.

Place the basin in a steamer or large saucepan half-filled with boiling water. Cover and cook for 1½ to 2 hours, topping up the water as necessary.

Remove the foil and turn the pudding out onto a plate. Serve with custard.

Serves 6

BANANA CRÊPES

BATTER:
125 g (4 oz) plain
   flour
pinch of salt
1 tablespoon icing
   sugar
1 tablespoon instant
   coffee powder
300 ml (½ pint)
   milk
1 tablespoon oil
1 egg
FILLING:
6 bananas
25 g (1 oz) butter,
   melted
2 tablespoons brandy
TO SERVE:
2 tablespoons flaked
   almonds, toasted
whipped cream

Place the batter ingredients in the blender or food processor and work until smooth.

Heat a 15 cm (6 inch) omelet pan and add a few drops of oil. Pour in 1 tablespoon batter, tilting the pan to coat the bottom evenly. Cook until the underside is brown, then turn and cook for 10 seconds. Repeat with the remaining batter, stacking the pancakes as they are cooked.

Cut the bananas in half lengthways and wrap each half in a pancake. Place in a shallow ovenproof dish, brush with the butter and pour over the brandy. Bake in a preheated moderate oven, 180°C (350°F), Gas Mark 4, for 15 minutes. Sprinkle with the almonds and serve with cream.
Serves 6

ORANGE AND RHUBARB PUDDING

500 g (1 lb) rhubarb
grated rind and juice
   of 1 orange
50 g (2 oz) soft
   brown sugar
PUDDING MIXTURE:
50 g (2 oz) soft
   margarine
50 g (2 oz) soft
   brown sugar
1 large egg
75 g (3 oz) self-
   raising flour, sifted
½ teaspoon baking
   powder
50 g (2 oz) almonds,
   chopped
TO SERVE:
Orange Cream (see
   left)

Cut the rhubarb into 2.5 cm (1 inch) lengths and place in a 900 ml (1½ pint) ovenproof dish. Pour over the orange juice and sprinkle with the orange rind and sugar.

Place all the pudding ingredients, except the almonds, in a bowl and beat thoroughly, using an electric beater, until combined.

Spoon over the rhubarb mixture and spread evenly to the edges. Sprinkle the almonds over the top and bake in a preheated moderate oven, 180°C (350°F), Gas Mark 4, for 35 to 40 minutes. Serve hot, with Orange Cream.
Serves 4

ORANGE CREAM

This is a good accompaniment to serve with pies and crumbles instead of cream.

250 g (8 oz) unsalted
   butter
300 ml (½ pint)
   milk
1 teaspoon gelatine
grated rind of 1
   orange
1 tablespoon caster
   sugar

Place all the ingredients in a pan and heat very gently until the butter has melted. Cool until lukewarm, then pour into the blender and blend on maximum speed for 30 seconds.

Chill in the refrigerator and whisk lightly before use. Or whisk stiffly and use for piping.
Makes 500 ml (18 fl oz)

BROWN BETTY

10 slices white bread,
 crusts removed
75 g (3 oz) butter
750 g-1 kg (1½-2lb)
 cooking apples,
 peeled, cored and
 sliced
75 g (3 oz) soft
 brown sugar

Spread the bread thickly with butter and cut each slice into 4. Butter a 1.5 litre (2½ pint) ovenproof dish generously and line with some of the bread, butter side down.

Cover with half the apples, sprinkle with sugar and arrange another layer of bread over the top. Cover with the remaining apples, sprinkle with sugar and top with the remaining bread, butter side up and slightly overlapping. Sprinkle with the remaining sugar.

Cover with foil and bake in a preheated moderate oven, 180°C (350°F), Gas Mark 4, for 35 minutes. Remove the foil and bake for a further 5 minutes until crisp and golden. Serve hot with custard or cream.
Serves 6

BREAD PUDDING

1 large white loaf
75 g (3 oz) shredded
 suet
350 g (12 oz) mixed
 dried fruit
50 g (2 oz) mixed
 peel
2 tablespoons mixed
 spice
1 tablespoon golden
 syrup
75 g (3 oz)
 margarine
125 g (4 oz) soft
 brown sugar
2 eggs, beaten
2 tablespoons
 demerara sugar

Slice the loaf, place in a large bowl and add just enough water to cover. Leave to soak for 30 minutes, then place in a colander and press out any excess water.

Transfer the bread to a mixing bowl and beat until smooth. Stir in the suet, fruit, peel, spice and syrup.

Cream together the margarine and soft brown sugar, then beat in the eggs. Add to the bread and mix well.

Turn into a greased ovenproof dish and sprinkle with the demerara sugar. Bake in a preheated moderately hot oven, 190°C (375°F), Gas Mark 5, for 1¼ to 1½ hours until firm and golden. Serve hot, with custard or cream.
Serves 6

OPPOSITE: *Banana Crêpes; Orange and Rhubarb Pudding; Orange Cream*
RIGHT: *Bread and Butter Pudding*

BREAD AND BUTTER PUDDING

9 slices white bread,
 crusts removed
50 g (2 oz) butter
50 g (2 oz) sultanas
 or currants
50 g (2 oz) caster
 sugar
2 large eggs
600 ml (1 pint) milk
grated nutmeg

Spread the bread thickly with butter and cut each slice into 4. Arrange half in a buttered 1.2 litre (2 pint) ovenproof dish, buttered side down. Sprinkle with the fruit and half the sugar. Cover with remaining bread, butter side up.

Beat the eggs and milk together and strain over the pudding. Sprinkle with the remaining sugar and nutmeg to taste and leave for 30 minutes.

Bake in a preheated moderate oven, 160°C (325°F), Gas Mark 3, for 50 to 60 minutes until the top is golden. Serve with custard or cream.
Serves 4

Apple Pancakes

APPLE PANCAKES

PANCAKES:
125 g (4 oz) plain
  flour
pinch of salt
1 egg, beaten
300 ml (½ pint)
  milk
1 tablespoon oil
FILLING:
25 g (1 oz) butter
750 g (1½ lb)
  cooking apples,
  peeled, cored and
  sliced
50 g (2 oz) brown
  sugar
½ teaspoon ground
  cinnamon
50 g (2 oz) sultanas
TO FINISH:
3 tablespoons apricot
  jam, warmed
25 g (1 oz) flaked
  almonds, toasted

Make and cook the pancakes as for Orange and Lemon Pancake Gâteau (see opposite).

Melt the butter in a pan. Add the apples, sugar, cinnamon and sultanas. Cover and simmer gently for 10 to 15 minutes, until the apples are tender.

Place a pancake on a greased ovenproof dish, cover with some of the apple mixture, then another pancake. Continue in this way until the apple mixture and pancakes are all used, finishing with a pancake.

Spoon over the apricot jam to glaze. Bake in a preheated moderate oven, 180°C (350°F), Gas Mark 4, for 10 to 15 minutes until heated through.

Cut into wedges and sprinkle with almonds. Serve with whipped cream if liked.
Serves 6

BANANA PANCAKE GÂTEAU

PANCAKES:
125 g (4 oz) plain
  flour
pinch of salt
1 egg
300 ml (½ pint) milk
oil for frying
FILLING & TOPPING:
4 bananas
113 g (4 oz) medium-
  fat curd cheese
1 teaspoon ground
  cinnamon
25 g (1 oz) soft
  brown sugar
2 tablespoons natural
  yogurt
250 g (8 oz)
  strawberries
1 tablespoon sherry
25 g (1 oz) sugar
juice of ½ lemon

Make and cook the pancakes as for Orange and Lemon Pancake Gâteau (see opposite). Keep warm while making the filling.

Mash 3 of the bananas with the cheese, cinnamon and brown sugar. Stir in the yogurt. Use the mixture to sandwich together the pancakes, stacking them one on top of the other on a warmed serving dish.

To make the sauce, sieve the strawberries or work in an electric blender until smooth. Stir in the sherry and sugar. Pour over the pancakes.

Slice the remaining banana and sprinkle with lemon juice. Arrange on top of the gâteau. Serve immediately, with cream.
Serves 4
NOTE: Fresh or frozen strawberries may be used for the topping.

DATE AND APPLE PANCAKES

PANCAKE BATTER:
125 g (4 oz)
  wholemeal flour
1 egg, beaten
300 ml (½ pint) milk
1 tablespoon oil
FILLING:
25 g (1 oz) margarine
500 g (1 lb) dessert
  apples, peeled,
  cored and sliced
25 g (1 oz)
  muscovado sugar
½ teaspoon ground
  mixed spice
75 g (3 oz) dates,
  chopped
TO FINISH:
2 tablespoons clear
  honey
25 g (1 oz) flaked
  almonds, roasted

Make and cook the pancakes as for Orange and Lemon Pancake Gâteau (see opposite).

Melt the margarine in a pan and add the apples, sugar, mixed spice and dates. Cook gently, stirring frequently, for 10 to 15 minutes until the apples are tender.

Place a little of the filling on each pancake, roll up and arrange in an ovenproof dish. Warm the honey and spoon over the pancakes to glaze. Bake in a preheated moderate oven, 180°C (350°F), Gas Mark 4, for 15 to 20 minutes until heated through.

Sprinkle with the almonds and serve with cream or natural yogurt.
Serves 4

ORANGE AND LEMON PANCAKE GÂTEAU

PANCAKES:
250 g (8 oz) plain flour
½ teaspoon salt
2 eggs, beaten
600 ml (1 pint) milk
½ teaspoon vanilla essence (optional)
oil for shallow frying

FILLING:
350 g (12 oz) sugar
5 tablespoons cornflour
¼ teaspoon salt
250 ml (8 fl oz) orange juice
6 tablespoons lemon juice
1 teaspoon grated lemon rind
25 g (1 oz) butter
5 egg yolks, beaten
icing sugar for sprinkling

To make the pancakes, sift the flour and salt into a bowl. Add the eggs and half the milk with the vanilla essence, if using. Beat until smooth. Gradually beat in the remaining milk.

Lightly grease an 18 cm (7 inch) frying pan and place over high heat. When very hot pour in just enough batter to coat the bottom. Cook until golden brown underneath, then turn the pancake and cook the other side. Repeat with the remaining batter to make about 20 pancakes, stacking them, interleaved with greaseproof paper, as they are cooked; keep warm.

To make the filling, put the sugar, cornflour and salt in a basin over a pan of simmering water. Gradually stir in the orange and lemon juices, then the lemon rind and butter. Heat gently, stirring, for 5 minutes. Cover with foil and continue heating, without stirring, for 10 minutes.

Remove the bowl from the pan and stir in the egg yolks. Return to the heat and cook for a further 2 minutes.

Use the filling to sandwich together the pancakes, stacking them one on top of the other. Cover the gâteau with foil and heat through in a preheated moderate oven, 160°C (325°F), Gas Mark 3, for 15 minutes.

Sprinkle with the icing sugar and serve cut into wedges.
Serves 8 to 10

APRICOT AND BANANA CRUMBLE

175 g (6 oz) dried apricots
6 large bananas, sliced
½ teaspoon ground coriander
175 g (6 oz) plain flour
75 g (3 oz) butter
75 g (3 oz) caster sugar

Soak the apricots in water to cover for 2 hours. Drain and chop. Put the apricots and bananas in a baking dish and sprinkle with the coriander.

Sift the flour into a bowl and rub in the butter until the mixture resembles breadcrumbs. Stir in the sugar. Sprinkle this topping over the fruit.

Cook in a preheated moderately hot oven, 200°C (400°F), Gas Mark 6, for 45 minutes or until the topping is golden brown. Serve with cream.
Serves 6

Orange and Lemon Pancake Gâteau; Apricot and Banana Crumble

RHUBARB AND APPLE COBBLER

500 g (1 lb) rhubarb, chopped
500 g (1 lb) cooking apples, peeled, cored and sliced
125 g (4 oz) caster sugar
1 teaspoon ground cinnamon
175 g (6 oz) self-raising flour
50 g (2 oz) butter or margarine
120 ml (4 fl oz) milk (approximately)

Put the rhubarb and apples in a saucepan with just enough water to cover the bottom of the pan. Add half the sugar and simmer for about 15 minutes until tender. Stir in the cinnamon and transfer to an ovenproof dish.

Sift the flour into a mixing bowl and rub in the fat until the mixture resembles breadcrumbs. Add the remaining sugar then stir in enough milk, a little at a time, to give a fairly soft dough.

Turn onto a lightly floured board and pat out to a 1 cm (½ inch) thickness. Cut into 3.5 cm (1½ inch) rounds, using a biscuit cutter, and arrange over the fruit.

Brush with milk and bake in a preheated moderately hot oven, 200°C (400°F), Gas Mark 6, for 15 minutes, or until the topping is golden.
Serves 4

SHERRY TRIFLE

1 packet of trifle sponges
3 tablespoons jam
3 egg yolks
2 teaspoons cornflour
25 g (1 oz) caster sugar
450 ml (¾ pint) milk
5 tablespoons sherry
2 bananas
142 ml (5 fl oz) double cream, whipped
TO DECORATE:
glacé cherries
angelica
blanched almonds, toasted

Split the sponge cakes in half, spread with jam and arrange in a glass serving bowl.

Beat the egg yolks with the cornflour and sugar until smooth. Bring the milk to the boil, pour onto the egg yolks and stir well.

Return to the pan and heat gently, stirring constantly, until the mixture is thick enough to coat the back of a wooden spoon. Cool slightly.

Sprinkle the sherry over the sponge cakes and slice the bananas over the top. Pour over the custard and leave until set.

Spread a layer of cream over the top. Decorate with piped cream rosettes, cherries, angelica and almonds.
Serves 4

GINGER RUM TRIFLE

1 × 227 g (8 oz) ginger cake, sliced
1 × 212 g (7½ oz) can pear quarters
6 tablespoons rum
300 ml (½ pint) cold thick custard
142 ml (5 fl oz) double cream
1-2 teaspoons icing sugar
flaked almonds, toasted, to decorate

Line a medium soufflé dish or glass bowl with half the ginger cake.

Drain the pears, reserving 2 tablespoons of the juice. Mix the rum with the reserved pear juice and sprinkle half over the cake. Place the pears on top, cover with the remaining cake and pour over the remaining rum mixture.

Spoon the custard over the cake. Whip the cream with the icing sugar until it forms soft peaks. Spoon over the custard and decorate with almonds.
Serves 4
NOTE: To make your own custard: beat 2 egg yolks with 2 teaspoons cornflour and 1 tablespoon caster sugar. Bring 300 ml (½ pint) milk to the boil, pour onto the egg yolks and stir well. Return to the pan and heat gently, stirring, until the mixture has thickened. Leave until cold and use as indicated.

APPLE FRITTERS

2 large cooking
   apples, peeled and
   cored
oil for deep-frying
icing sugar for
   dredging
FRITTER BATTER:
50 g (2 oz) plain
   flour
1 egg, separated
4 tablespoons water
1 teaspoon oil

First make the fritter batter: place the flour, egg yolk, water and oil in an electric blender or food processor and work until smooth. Pour into a bowl. Whisk the egg white until stiff and fold into the batter.

Cut the apple into 5mm (¼ inch) slices. Dip the apples in the batter, draining off any excess, then deep-fry in hot oil for 2 to 3 minutes until golden.

Drain on kitchen paper, dredge with icing sugar and serve with cream.

Serves 4

NOTE: To test oil for frying fritters, heat the oil in a deep-fryer until a cube of bread turns golden and rises to the surface immediately it is dropped in the pan.

APPLE AND SULTANA FRITTERS

2 × quantity fritter
   batter (see recipe)
4 dessert apples,
   peeled, cored and
   finely chopped or
   grated
juice of ½ lemon
2 teaspoons caster
   sugar
25 g (1 oz) sultanas
oil for deep-frying, or
   butter for shallow-
   frying
caster sugar and
   cinnamon to serve

Make the fritter batter (see Apple Fritters, above). Mix together the apple, lemon juice, sugar and sultanas; fold into the batter.

If deep-frying, heat the oil in a deep-fryer and test (see Apple Fritters, above). Drop dessert-spoonfuls of the mixture into the oil and fry for 2 to 3 minutes until crisp and golden brown. If shallow-frying, melt the butter in a pan and fry for 4 to 5 minutes on each side.

Drain well and keep hot, while cooking the remaining mixture. Sprinkle with sugar and cinnamon and serve hot.

Serves 4 to 6

VARIATIONS: Replace the apple with chopped banana or pineapple.

OPPOSITE: *Rhubarb and Apple Cobbler*
RIGHT: *Apple Fritters; Apple and Orange Flan (see page 99)*

SPECIAL OCCASION DESSERTS

Whenever you are entertaining, it is well worth spending a little extra time and effort on the dessert, for this is the course which usually brings more compliments than any other! Don't feel restricted to choosing from this chapter; you will find plenty of desserts suitable for special occasions throughout the book – especially amongst the soufflés, mousses, cheesecakes and fruit desserts. Most of the recipes in this section take a little longer to prepare, but the results are certainly rewarding.

The spectacular bombes and ice cream gâteaux can, of course, be prepared well ahead and stored in the freezer until required. Similarly the delicious charlottes, elaborate cream gâteaux and little summer puddings can be made in advance; for optimum appearance apply the decoration an hour or so before serving. Shortcake rounds and choux buns for profiteroles can be made the day before they are required, but these cream-filled desserts are best assembled shortly before serving.

Whatever the occasion, make sure you choose the right dessert to complement the rest of the meal. Follow a rich main course with a light fluffy dessert or sorbet. Sumptuous gâteaux taste wonderfully decadent after a light main course. If you choose to serve a rich, creamy dessert, it is worthwhile having some fresh fruit to hand or even preparing a simple fruit salad for those guests with smaller appetites – if you have time on the day.

Raspberry Charlotte

RASPBERRY CHARLOTTE

350 g (12 oz)
  raspberries
2 eggs
1 egg yolk
75 g (3 oz) caster
  sugar
15 g (½ oz) gelatine,
  soaked in
  3 tablespoons
  cold water
284 ml (10 fl oz)
  double cream,
  lightly whipped
30 Langue de Chat
  biscuits (see page
  149)

Set aside about 8 raspberries for decoration. Purée the remainder in an electric blender or food processor then sieve to remove the pips.

Place the eggs, egg yolk and sugar in a bowl and whisk with an electric mixer until thick and mousse-like. Meanwhile, heat the gelatine gently until dissolved, then mix into the purée; cool slightly. Carefully fold the purée and two thirds of the cream into the mousse.

Stir over a bowl of iced water until beginning to set, then turn into a greased 18 cm (7 inch) loose-bottomed cake tin. Chill until set.

Turn out onto a serving dish. Spread a little of the remaining cream round the sides and press on the biscuits, overlapping slightly.

Decorate with the remaining cream and raspberries.
Serves 8

INDIVIDUAL SUMMER PUDDINGS

500 g (1 lb) mixed
  blackberries,
  blackcurrants and
  redcurrants
75 g (3 oz) caster
  sugar
4 tablespoons water
125 g (4 oz)
  strawberries, sliced
125 g (4 oz)
  raspberries
16 slices white bread,
  crusts removed
TO DECORATE:
8 tablespoons double
  cream, whipped
few sprigs of
  redcurrants or
  blackcurrants
  (optional)

Place the blackberries and currants in a heavy pan with the sugar and water. Cook gently, stirring occasionally, for 10 minutes, until tender. Add the strawberries and raspberries and leave to cool. Strain, reserving the juice.

Cut out sixteen 7.5 cm (3 inch) circles of bread. Cut the remaining bread into 2.5 cm (1 inch) wide strips. Soak in the reserved juice.

Line the bases of 8 ramekin dishes with the circles of bread. Arrange the strips to fit around the sides. Divide the fruit between the dishes and place the remaining circles on top.

Cover each dish with greaseproof paper and stand one on top of another on 2 saucers. Place a cup containing a 250 g (8 oz) weight on a saucer on top of each pile to weigh down. Leave overnight in the refrigerator.

Turn out onto individual plates and decorate with whipped cream and currants, if desired.
Serves 8

FREEZING STRAWBERRIES

Strawberries are available in abundance from May to June. It is worth freezing them for later use as out of season they are expensive and often lack flavour. Although they keep their flavour when frozen, whole strawberries tend to lose their water and texture. Consequently it is more successful to freeze sliced or crushed strawberries. Only freeze ripe, fresh and uncrushed fruit without any traces of mould. Cut the fruit into 3 or 4 slices, or alternatively mash lightly with a fork.

To freeze slices, pack in rigid containers and cover with a sugar syrup made by dissolving 350 g (12 oz) sugar in 600 ml (1 pint) water; sweeten crushed fruit to taste and pack in rigid containers, leaving 2 cm (¾ inch) headspace. Seal, label and freeze for up to 12 months.

To thaw, leave to stand in container at room temperature for about 1½ hours. Use strawberry slices in fruit salads; drain and use as a dessert topping or incorporate in Individual Summer Puddings (see above). Use crushed strawberries in ices, sorbets and mousses.

CREAM CHEESE MOUSSE WITH STRAWBERRIES

227 g (8 oz) curd cheese
2 egg yolks
50 g (2 oz) caster sugar
½ teaspoon vanilla essence
15 g (½ oz) gelatine, soaked in 3 table-spoons cold water
284 ml (10 fl oz) whipping cream, whipped
350 g (12 oz) strawberries, halved
2 tablespoons Cointreau

Place the cheese in a bowl with the egg yolks, sugar and vanilla essence and beat until smooth. Heat the gelatine gently until dissolved, then mix into the cheese mixture with the cream.

Turn into an oiled 900 ml (1½ pint) ring mould and chill until set.

Sprinkle the strawberries with the liqueur and leave to soak for 1 hour.

Turn the mousse out onto a serving plate and fill the centre with the strawberries.
Serves 6

STRAWBERRY AND ALMOND SHORTCAKE

75 g (3 oz) butter
50 g (2 oz) caster sugar
75 g (3 oz) ground almonds, toasted
125 g (4 oz) plain flour
egg white for brushing
1 tablespoon chopped almonds
250 g (8 oz) strawberries, sliced
284 ml (10 fl oz) double cream, whipped
2 tablespoons Cointreau

Beat the butter and sugar together until light and fluffy. Stir in the almonds and flour and mix to a firm dough, using your hand. Divide in half and roll each piece into a 20 cm (8 inch) round on a baking sheet. Brush one round with egg white and sprinkle with the chopped almonds.

Bake in a preheated moderate oven, 180°C (350°F), Gas Mark 4, for 15 to 20 minutes until golden. Cut the nut-covered round into 8 sections while still warm. Cool on a wire rack.

Reserve 8 strawberry slices and a little cream. Fold the Cointreau and remaining strawberries and cream together; spread over the almond round. Arrange the triangles at an angle on top and decorate with the reserved strawberries and cream.
Serves 8

Cream Cheese Mousse with Strawberries; Strawberry and Almond Shortcake

SUMMER SOUFFLÉ

250 g (8 oz) raspberries
250 g (8 oz) strawberries
4 eggs, separated
75 g (3 oz) caster sugar
15 g (½ oz) gelatine, soaked in 2 tablespoons orange juice
284 ml (10 fl oz) double cream, whipped
TO FINISH:
15 g (½ oz) ratafias, crushed
4 tablespoons double cream, whipped

Tie a band of double greaseproof paper around a 1 litre (1¾ pint) soufflé dish to stand 5 cm (2 inches) above the rim; oil the inside of the paper.

Reserve 8 raspberries for decoration. Work the remainder with the strawberries in an electric blender or food processor to make approximately 250 ml (8 fl oz) purée; sieve to remove pips.

Place the egg yolks and sugar in a bowl and whisk with an electric mixer until thick. Heat the gelatine gently until dissolved. Add to the fruit purée, then carefully fold into the egg mixture with the cream.

Whisk the egg whites until stiff. Fold into the mousse when it begins to set. Turn into the dish and chill in the refrigerator until set.

Remove the paper carefully and press the ratafia crumbs around the side. Decorate with piped cream and the reserved raspberries.
Serves 6 to 8

ORANGE SYLLABUB IN LACE BASKETS

grated rind and juice of 2 oranges
2 tablespoons Grand Marnier
284 ml (10 fl oz) double cream
2 egg whites
50 g (2 oz) caster sugar
8 Lace Baskets (see page 148)
finely shredded orange rind to decorate

Place the orange rind and juice in a bowl with the liqueur.

Whip the cream until it stands in peaks, then gradually add the orange mixture and continue whisking until it holds its shape.

Whisk the egg whites until stiff, then whisk in the sugar. Carefully fold into the cream mixture.

Spoon carefully into the Lace Baskets and sprinkle with orange rind.
Serves 8

LOGANBERRY FOOL

300 g (10 oz) loganberries
75 g (3 oz) caster sugar
284 ml (10 fl oz) whipping cream, whipped

Set aside 6 loganberries for decoration. Place the rest in an electric blender or food processor with the sugar and work to a purée. Sieve to remove the pips.

Fold into the cream, spoon into individual glasses and chill. Decorate with a loganberry and serve with Nutty Curls (see page 148) if desired.
Serves 6

SUMMER FRUIT WHIRL

175 g (6 oz) strawberries, halved
175 g (6 oz) raspberries
1 tablespoon caster sugar
2 tablespoons brandy
8 meringue shells
284 ml (10 fl oz) double cream, whipped

Place the strawberries and raspberries in a bowl and sprinkle with the sugar and brandy. Leave to soak for 1 hour. Break the meringues into small pieces and fold into the cream.

Spoon one third of the fruit into 6 glasses. Cover with half the cream mixture. Repeat the layers, finishing with a layer of fruit. Serve chilled.
Serves 6
NOTE: To make meringue shells, follow recipe for Meringue Suisse (see page 82).

CIDER SYLLABUB

284 ml (10 fl oz) double cream
grated rind and juice of 1 lemon
120 ml (4 fl oz) sweet cider
2 egg whites
50 g (2 oz) caster sugar

Put the cream and lemon rind in a bowl and whisk until thick. Gradually add the lemon juice and cider and continue whisking until it holds its shape.

Whisk the egg whites until stiff. Whisk in the sugar, then carefully fold in the cream mixture.

Spoon into glasses and serve with Almond Curls (see page 151).
Serves 6

Summer Soufflé; Loganberry Fool; Summer Fruit Whirl

MOCHA ROULADE

175 g (6 oz) plain
  chocolate
3 tablespoons water
1 tablespoon instant
  coffee powder
5 eggs, separated
250 g (8 oz) caster
  sugar
FILLING:
1 tablespoon instant
  coffee powder
1 tablespoon boiling
  water
284 ml (10 fl oz)
  double cream,
  whipped
1 tablespoon icing
  sugar
TO FINISH:
sifted icing sugar

Place the chocolate, water and coffee in a pan and heat gently until the chocolate has melted. Beat the egg yolks with the caster sugar until thick and creamy, then fold in the warm chocolate mixture.

Whisk the egg whites until stiff and fold into the chocolate mixture. Turn into a lined and greased 20 × 30 cm (8 × 12 inch) Swiss roll tin. Bake in a preheated moderate oven, 180°C (350°F), Gas Mark 4, for 20 to 25 minutes until firm.

Leave for 5 minutes, cover with a damp cloth and leave until cool. Place in the refrigerator overnight.

Carefully remove the cloth and turn the roulade out onto a sheet of greaseproof paper, sprinkled thickly with icing sugar. Peel off the lining paper.

Dissolve the coffee in the water, cool, then fold into the cream with the sugar. Spread evenly over the roulade and roll up like a Swiss roll. Transfer to a serving plate.
Serves 8

CHOCOLATE AND RUM CHARLOTTE

1½ packets sponge
  fingers
4 tablespoons rum
100 g (3½ oz) plain
  chocolate
75 g (3 oz) light soft
  brown sugar
125 g (4 oz) unsalted
  butter, softened
2 eggs, separated
TO DECORATE:
rose leaves, washed
  and thoroughly
  dried
50 g (2 oz) plain
  chocolate, melted
142 ml (5 fl oz)
  double cream,
  whipped

Dip each sponge finger into the rum and use to line the base and sides of an 18 cm (6 inch) soufflé dish, sugar side out.

Melt the chocolate in a basin over hot water. Cream the sugar and butter until light, then stir in the chocolate while still hot. Beat in the egg yolks, then fold in the stiffly whisked egg whites. Pour into the soufflé dish and chill for 24 hours.

To prepare the leaves, paint the undersides with melted chocolate. Leave until set, then carefully peel each leaf away from the chocolate.

Before turning out the charlotte, trim the sponge fingers to the level of the chocolate filling. Invert onto a serving plate and decorate with the whipped cream and chocolate leaves.
Serves 6

CHOCOLATE AND CHESTNUT MOULD

250 g (8 oz) plain
  chocolate, broken
  into pieces
4 tablespoons water
125 g (4 oz) butter
125 g (4 oz) caster
  sugar
2 × 227 g (8 oz)
  cans unsweetened
  chestnut purée
2 tablespoons brandy
142 ml (5 fl oz)
  double cream,
  whipped, to
  decorate

Place the chocolate and water in a small pan and heat gently until melted, then allow to cool.

Cream the butter and sugar together until light and fluffy, then gradually add the chestnut purée, beating well between each addition. Stir in the melted chocolate and brandy. Turn into a greased 900 ml (1½ pint) mould. Leave in the refrigerator overnight.

Turn out onto a serving dish and decorate with piped cream.
Serves 8
(Illustrated on page 66)

LEFT: *Mocha Roulade*
OPPOSITE: *Rum and Blackcurrant Torten; Tipsy Mandarin Torten*

RUM AND BLACKCURRANT TORTEN

CAKE MIXTURE:
75 g (3 oz) self-raising flour
3 tablespoons cocoa powder
4 eggs
75 g (3 oz) caster sugar
TO FINISH:
2 tablespoons dark rum
4 tablespoons blackcurrant conserve
284 ml (10 fl oz) double cream, whipped
50 g (2 oz) flaked almonds, toasted
2-3 teaspoons cocoa powder, sifted, for sprinkling

First make two 23 cm (9 inch) cakes as for Tipsy Mandarin Torten (see right). Cool on a wire rack.

Place one sponge on a cake board and drizzle over half the rum. Leave for about 10 minutes until absorbed, then spread with 3 tablespoons of the conserve and one third of the cream. Place the other sponge on top and drizzle over the remaining rum; leave for 10 minutes.

Reserve 3 tablespoons of the remaining cream for decoration; use the rest to coat the top and side of the cake. Press the almonds onto the side of the cake. Chill for 30 minutes.

Lightly mark the top into 12 sections. Using a piping bag fitted with a star nozzle, pipe an open rosette of cream on each portion and fill with the remaining conserve. Dust the centre of the cake with cocoa powder.
Serves 12

TIPSY MANDARIN TORTEN

CAKE MIXTURE:
75 g (3 oz) self-raising flour
3 tablespoons cocoa powder
4 eggs
75 g (3 oz) caster sugar
TO FINISH:
2 tablespoons Grand Marnier
1 tablespoon tangerine or mild orange marmalade
284 ml (10 fl oz) double cream, whipped
16-18 Langue de Chat biscuits (see page 149), trimmed
1 × 312 g (11 oz) can mandarin segments, drained
50 g (2 oz) plain chocolate, grated

Sift flour and cocoa together twice. Whisk the eggs and sugar together in a large bowl until the whisk leaves a trail. Fold in the flour mixture. Divide between two greased and floured 23 cm (9 inch) cake tins and bake in a preheated moderately hot oven, 200°C (400°F), Gas Mark 6, for 15 to 20 minutes or until springy to the touch. Cool on a wire rack.

Place one sponge on a serving plate and drizzle over half the liqueur. Leave for 10 minutes, then spread with the marmalade and about one third of the cream. Place the other sponge on top and drizzle over the remaining liqueur. Leave for 10 minutes. Cover the top and side of the cake with the remaining cream and chill for 30 minutes.

Lightly mark the top into 12 sections. Press the biscuits around the side of the cake. Decorate with the mandarins and grated chocolate.
Serves 12

GÂTEAU AUX NOIX

MERINGUE:
4 egg whites
250 g (8 oz) caster sugar
125 g (4 oz) walnut halves, ground

FILLING:
125 g (4 oz) sugar
4 tablespoons water
4 tablespoons hot black coffee
426 ml (15 fl oz) double cream, whipped

TO FINISH:
sifted icing sugar
8 walnut halves

Whisk the egg whites until stiff, then whisk in 2 tablespoons of the caster sugar. Carefully fold in the remaining sugar with the walnuts.

Put the meringue into a piping bag, fitted with a 1 cm (½ inch) plain nozzle, and pipe into two 20 cm (8 inch) rounds on baking sheets lined with silicone paper. Bake in a preheated cool oven, 140°C (275°F), Gas Mark 1, for 1½ to 2 hours. Transfer to a wire rack to cool.

Place the sugar and water in a pan and heat gently until dissolved. Increase the heat and cook to a rich brown caramel. Remove from the heat, carefully add the coffee and stir until the caramel has melted, heating again if necessary, then cool.

Fold the cream into the caramel and use three-quarters to sandwich the meringue rounds together. Sprinkle the top with icing sugar. Pipe cream rosettes around the edge and decorate with walnut halves.

Serves 6

HAZELNUT GALETTE

HAZELNUT PASTRY:
75 g (3 oz) butter
50 g (2 oz) caster sugar
125 g (4 oz) plain flour, sifted
75 g (3 oz) hazelnuts, ground and toasted

FILLING:
1 tablespoon apricot jam
500 g (1 lb) dessert apples, peeled, cored and sliced
25 g (1 oz) sultanas
25 g (1 oz) currants
1 teaspoon ground mixed spice
142 ml (5 fl oz) double cream, whipped

TO FINISH:
sifted icing sugar
8 hazelnuts, toasted and skinned

Beat the butter and sugar together until light and fluffy. Stir in the flour and hazelnuts and mix to a firm dough, using one hand. Turn onto a floured surface and knead lightly until smooth. Divide the mixture in half and roll each piece into a 20 cm (8 inch) round on a baking sheet.

Bake in a preheated moderately hot oven, 190°C (375°F), Gas Mark 5, for 15 to 20 minutes until golden. Cut one round into 8 sections while still warm. Transfer both rounds to a wire rack to cool.

Place the jam and apples in a pan, cover and cook gently for 15 to 20 minutes until softened, stirring occasionally. Add the sultanas, currants and spice. Leave until cool.

Spread the cooled apple mixture over the hazelnut round. Cover with half the cream. Arrange the hazelnut sections on top and sprinkle with icing sugar. Pipe a cream rosette on each section and top with hazelnuts.

Serves 8

RASPBERRY HAZELNUT MERINGUE

4 egg whites
275 g (9 oz) caster
  sugar
few drops of vanilla
  essence
1 teaspoon vinegar
125 g (4 oz) ground
  hazelnuts, toasted
FILLING:
284 ml (10 fl oz)
  double cream,
  whipped
1 tablespoon caster
  sugar
250 g (8 oz)
  raspberries
TO FINISH:
sifted icing sugar

Whisk the egg whites until stiff, then whisk in the sugar, a tablespoon at a time. Continue whisking until the meringue is very stiff and holds its shape. Carefully fold in the vanilla essence, vinegar and hazelnuts.

Divide the mixture between two lined and greased 20 cm (8 inch) sandwich tins and spread evenly. Bake in a preheated moderate oven, 180°C (350°F), Gas Mark 4, for 40 to 45 minutes.

Loosen from the tin with a sharp knife and turn onto a wire rack to cool.

To make the filling: mix two thirds of the cream with the sugar and raspberries, reserving a few for decoration. Sandwich the meringue rounds together with the filling and dust the top with icing sugar.

Decorate with piped cream rosettes and the reserved raspberries.
Serves 6

BLACK FOREST GÂTEAU

SPONGE MIXTURE:
3 large eggs
75 g (3 oz) caster
  sugar
50 g (2 oz) plain
  flour
1 tablespoon cocoa
  powder
1 tablespoon oil
TO FINISH:
1 × 425 g (15 oz)
  can black cherries
1 tablespoon
  arrowroot
3 tablespoons kirsch
284 ml (10 fl oz)
  double cream,
  whipped
chocolate curls (see
  below)

Place the eggs and sugar in a bowl and whisk over a pan of simmering water until thick and mousse-like. Sift the flour with the cocoa and fold in, then fold in the oil.

Turn into a lined and greased 20 cm (8 inch) round cake tin. Bake in a preheated moderately hot oven, 190°C (375°F), Gas Mark 5, for 30 to 35 minutes. Cool on a wire rack.

Drain the cherries and mix a little of the juice with the arrowroot in a small bowl. Pour the remaining juice into a pan and bring to the boil. Pour onto the arrowroot and stir well. Return to the pan and heat gently, stirring until thick and clear. Stone the cherries, add to the pan and cool.

Slice the cake in half horizontally and sprinkle both layers with kirsch. Place one layer on a plate, and pipe a line of cream around the top edge. Spread the cherry mixture in the centre and top with the other layer.

Spread half the remaining cream around the side of the gâteau and press chocolate curls into it. Pipe the remaining cream on top of the gâteau.
Serves 6

CHOCOLATE DECORATIONS

To make chocolate decorations, spread a thin even layer of melted chocolate on a piece of foil or greaseproof paper. Leave until just set, but not too hard.

Cut into squares using a sharp knife and a ruler. To make triangles, cut the squares in half. To make long-sided triangles, cut the chocolate into rectangles, then cut in half. When hard, carefully lift the tip of the paper and peel away from the chocolate. To make circles, cut the chocolate into small rounds, using a pastry cutter.

To make chocolate caraque: using a sharp, thin-bladed knife at a slight angle, push the knife across the chocolate with a slight sawing movement, scraping off a thin layer. This will form a long scroll.

Curls can be made by peeling layers straight from a block of chocolate with a potato peeler. The chocolate must not be too cold or it will not curl satisfactorily.

OPPOSITE: *Gâteau aux Noix; Hazelnut Galette*
RIGHT: *Black Forest Gâteau*

TARTUFI

125 g (4 oz) plain
chocolate, chopped
2 teaspoons instant
coffee powder
2 tablespoons water
2 tablespoons dark
rum
284 ml (10 fl oz)
double cream
75 g (3 oz) blanched
almonds, chopped
and toasted
6 chocolate rose
leaves (see page
127) to decorate

Place the chocolate and coffee in a pan with the water. Heat very gently until melted. Add the rum and leave to cool.

Whip the cream until thick and fold in the chocolate mixture and almonds. Spoon into individual dishes and decorate with chocolate rose leaves. Serve chilled.

Serves 6

NUTTY PROFITEROLES WITH BUTTERSCOTCH SAUCE

CHOUX PASTRY:
50 g (2 oz) butter
150 ml (¼ pint)
water
65 g (2½ oz) plain
flour, sifted
2 eggs, beaten
50 g (2 oz) blanched
almonds, chopped
FILLING:
175 ml (6 fl oz)
double cream
2 tablespoons Tia
Maria
Butterscotch Sauce
(see page 153)

Melt the butter in a large pan, add the water and bring to the boil. Add the flour all at once and beat until the mixture leaves the side of the pan. Cool slightly, then add the eggs a little at a time, beating vigorously.

Put the mixture into a piping bag fitted with a plain 1 cm (½ inch) nozzle and pipe small mounds on a dampened baking sheet. Sprinkle with the almonds.

Bake in a preheated hot oven, 220°C (425°F), Gas Mark 7, for 10 minutes, then lower the heat to 190°C (375°F), Gas Mark 5, and bake for a further 20 to 25 minutes, until golden. Make a slit in the side of each bun and cool on a wire rack.

Whip the cream with the liqueur until stiff. Spoon a little into each bun. Pile the profiteroles on a serving dish and pour over the warm butterscotch sauce to serve.

Serves 4 to 6

CHOCOLATE CHERRY SHORTCAKE

125 g (4 oz) butter
50 g (2 oz) caster
sugar
150 g (5 oz) plain
flour, sifted
25 g (1 oz) cocoa,
sifted
284 ml (10 fl oz)
double cream,
whipped
350 g (12 oz) fresh
or canned black
cherries, stoned
sifted icing sugar for
sprinkling

Cream the butter and sugar together until soft and creamy, then stir in the flour and cocoa. Mix to a firm dough, turn onto a floured surface and knead lightly. Divide the mixture in half and roll each piece into a 20 cm (8 inch) round on a baking sheet.

Bake in a preheated moderate oven, 180°C (350°F), Gas Mark 4, for 20 minutes. Leave for 2 minutes, then cut one round into 8 sections. Carefully slide both rounds onto a wire rack to cool.

Reserve 2 tablespoons of the cream. Mix the rest with the cherries and spread over the chocolate round.

Arrange the cut sections on top and sprinkle with icing sugar. Decorate with the reserved cream.

Serves 8

MOCHA HAZELNUT TORTE

75 g (3 oz) plain
chocolate
3 tablespoons water
50 g (2 oz) butter
50 g (2 oz) soft light
brown sugar
1 egg yolk
50 g (2 oz)
hazelnuts, toasted
and ground
2 tablespoons dark
rum
4 tablespoons strong
black coffee
16 sponge fingers
284 ml (10 fl oz)
double cream,
whipped
hazelnuts to decorate

Place the chocolate and water in a small pan and heat gently until melted; leave to cool.

Cream the butter and sugar together until light and fluffy. Add the egg yolk and beat thoroughly. Beat in the cooled chocolate and ground hazelnuts.

Mix the rum and coffee together; dip in the sponge fingers, and use half to cover the base of a lined and greased 500 g (1 lb) loaf tin.

Spread a quarter of the cream on top, then cover with the chocolate mixture. Spread one third of the remaining cream on top and cover with the remaining sponge fingers. Chill in the refrigerator until set.

Turn out onto a serving plate, pipe the remaining cream on top and decorate with hazelnuts.

Serves 6 to 8

Chocolate Cherry Shortcake; Mocha Hazelnut Torte; Tartufi

MERINGUE GLACÉ AUX ANANAS

MERINGUE:
4 egg whites
*250 g (8 oz) caster
 sugar*
FILLING:
*½ quantity Pine-
 apple Ice Cream
 (see page 35)*
*284 ml (10 fl oz)
 double cream*
*50 g (2 oz) preserved
 ginger, thinly
 sliced*
*2 tablespoons ginger
 syrup*
TO DECORATE:
*3 tablespoons double
 cream, whipped*
*15 g (½ oz)
 preserved ginger,
 sliced*

Make the meringue, pipe and cook
three 15 cm (6 inch) rounds as for
Vacherin aux Marrons (see page 91).

Remove the pineapple ice cream
from the freezer and allow to thaw
for 10 minutes at room temperature.

Whip the cream until it forms soft
peaks. Fold in the ginger and syrup.

Line a 20 cm (8 inch) cake tin with
a layer of pineapple ice. Place a
meringue round on top and cover
with half the ginger cream. Repeat
these layers and top with the third
meringue round, filling the space at
the sides with pineapple ice cream.
Cover with foil and freeze for 3 to
4 hours.

Transfer to the refrigerator 1 hour
before serving to soften. Turn out
onto a serving dish and decorate with
piped cream and ginger.
Serves 8

BOMBE AU CHOCOLAT

CHOCOLATE ICE
 CREAM:
2 eggs
2 egg yolks
*75 g (3 oz) caster
 sugar*
*426 ml (15 fl oz)
 single cream*
*250 g (8 oz) plain
 chocolate, chopped*
*284 ml (10 fl oz)
 double cream*
FILLING:
1 tablespoon rum
*1 tablespoon icing
 sugar*
*142 ml (5 fl oz)
 double cream,
 whipped*
3 bananas, sliced

Make the chocolate ice cream (see
page 31) and freeze until firm.

Add the rum and icing sugar to the
cream and fold in the bananas.

Line the sides of a chilled 1.5 litre
(2½ pint) bombe mould or
freezerproof basin thickly with the
chocolate ice cream. Fill the centre
with the banana filling and cover with
any remaining ice cream. Put on the
lid of the bombe mould or cover the
basin with foil and freeze for 4 hours.

Dip the mould or basin into cold
water and turn the bombe out onto a
chilled serving dish.
Serves 6 to 8

Meringue Glacé aux Ananas; Bombe au Chocolat

CHOCOLATE AND ORANGE SLICE

ORANGE ICE CREAM:
finely grated rind and juice of 2 oranges
3 eggs, separated
150 g (5 oz) caster sugar
284 ml (10 fl oz) double cream, lightly whipped
CHOCOLATE LAYER:
125 g (4 oz) plain chocolate, chopped
4 tablespoons single cream
TO FINISH:
142 ml (5 fl oz) double cream, whipped
chocolate rose leaves (see below)

Put the orange rind, egg yolks and half the sugar in a bowl. Whisk with an electric mixer until thick. Whisk the egg whites until stiff; gradually whisk in the remaining sugar.

Whisk the orange juice into the whipped cream. Fold into the egg mixture, then fold into the meringue mixture. Turn into a rigid freezerproof container, cover, seal and freeze until firm.

Place the chocolate and cream in a small pan and heat gently until the chocolate has melted; cool.

Spread half the ice cream in a 1 kg (2 lb) loaf tin evenly. Spread the chocolate mixture smoothly over the top and freeze for 20 minutes. Return remaining ice cream to the freezer.

When the chocolate layer has set, carefully spread the remaining ice cream on top and smooth. Cover with foil, seal and freeze until firm.

Turn out onto a serving plate and decorate with cream and rose leaves.
Serves 8

Chocolate and Orange Slice

TO MAKE CHOCOLATE ROSE LEAVES

When making chocolate decorations, chocolate cake covering or plain chocolate give the best results. To make chocolate rose leaves, pick fresh, undamaged leaves with clearly marked veins. Wash them thoroughly and dry carefully. Break the chocolate into small pieces and place in a basin over a pan of hot water. Heat gently until the chocolate melts, taking care not to let any water get into the chocolate; do not overheat. Coat the underside of each leaf with melted chocolate using a fine paintbrush, and making sure the chocolate is spread evenly to the edges.

Allow to set in a cool place, chocolate side up. Do not leave to set in the refrigerator or they will set with a dull finish. When hard, carefully lift the tip of the rose leaf and peel away from the chocolate. It is advisable to handle these decorations carefully because they are delicate. Make more than you require to allow for breakages.

Chocolate rose leaves and other chocolate decorations can be stored in an airtight container for several weeks.

RASPBERRY BOMBE

250 g (8 oz) raspberries
3 tablespoons icing sugar
284 ml (10 fl oz) double cream
142 ml (5 fl oz) single cream
125 g (4 oz) meringues
raspberries to decorate (optional)

Place the raspberries and icing sugar in an electric blender or food processor and blend until smooth; sieve to remove the pips.

Whip the double and single creams together until they form soft peaks. Break the meringues into pieces and fold into the cream.

Very lightly fold half the raspberry purée into the cream mixture to give a marbled effect. Turn into a 1.2 litre (2 pint) pudding basin, cover with foil, seal and freeze until firm.

Turn out onto a serving plate and place in the refrigerator 40 minutes before serving to soften. Pour the remaining purée over the bombe to serve. Decorate with fresh raspberries if desired.
Serves 6
NOTE: to make meringues, see recipe for Meringue Suisse (page 82).

CONTINENTAL DESSERTS

This exciting chapter presents an irresistible collection of desserts from the continent – especially French, Italian and Austrian favourites. Choose from fruit-filled French crêpes, refreshing Italian ices and Austrian pâtisserie, for example. Many of the recipes – including Austrian Curd Cake (page 139), Italian Curd Tart (page 143) and French Apple Flan (page 142) can be served with coffee, at teatime or as a dessert.

In France, the dessert course normally only comes into its own on special occasions. At other times, a light creamy dessert or fresh fruit is usually served. Crêpes are popular throughout France but they originated in Brittany. Traditionally made from buckwheat flour, they are paper-thin and served simply sprinkled with sugar or liqueur, spread with jam or stuffed with sweet mixtures. These crêpes are absolutely delicious – served as a dessert or as a filling snack at any time of the day.

Italians normally finish a meal with fresh fruit and cheese, rather than a dessert. Probably the only exception to this are those occasions when *gelati* and *granite* – ice creams and water ices – are served. Italy is, of course, famous for its delicious ices. Indeed it is the Italians we have to thank for the invention of ice cream as we know it today. The mouth-watering Italian Hazelnut Ice (page 134), Amaretti Ice Cream (page 132) and Orange Granita (page 132) are a far cry from the ancient Romans' water ice which was simply a mixture of ice from the mountains and crushed fruit!

MONT BLANC

2 egg whites
125 g (4 oz) caster
    sugar
½ teaspoon vanilla
    essence
FILLING:
142 ml (5 fl oz)
    double cream
1 tablespoon icing
    sugar
1 × 227 g (8 oz) can
    sweetened chestnut
    purée
1 tablespoon brandy
25 g (1 oz) plain
    chocolate, grated

Whisk the egg whites until stiff.
Gradually whisk in the caster sugar
and ¼ teaspoon vanilla essence.
Spoon the meringue into a piping bag
fitted with a 1 cm (½ inch) plain
nozzle. Draw 4 circles 7.5 cm
(3 inches) in diameter onto baking
sheets lined with non-stick paper and
cover with the meringue.

Bake in a preheated very cool oven,
120°C (250°F), Gas Mark ½, for
about 1¼ hours, until firm but not
browned. Cool. Arrange on serving
plates.

Whip the cream until it forms soft
peaks, then fold in the icing sugar and
remaining vanilla essence.

Mix the chestnut purée with the
brandy. Spoon into a piping bag
fitted with a 3 mm (⅛ inch) plain
nozzle and pipe around the edge of
the meringue bases. Top with the
cream and chocolate. Serve chilled.
Serves 4

MOUSSE À L'ORANGE

6 eggs, separated
175 g (6 oz) caster
    sugar
3 tablespoons
    Cointreau
grated rind and juice
    of 4 oranges
15 g (½ oz) gelatine
2 tablespoons water
142 ml (5 fl oz)
    double cream,
    lightly whipped
mint leaves to
    decorate

Put the egg yolks and sugar in a bowl
over a pan of hot water and whisk
until thick and creamy. Gradually
whisk in the Cointreau, orange rind
and juice. Continue whisking until
the mixture is thick. Remove from
the heat and allow to cool slightly.

Put the gelatine and water in a
bowl over a pan of hot water and stir
until dissolved. Add to the orange
mixture. Fold in the cream. Whisk
the egg whites until stiff and fold into
the orange mixture.

Spoon into individual dishes and
chill until set.

Decorate with mint to serve.
Serves 6
NOTE: For a professional finish, serve
the mousse in scooped-out orange
shells.

GLACE AU CAFÉ

142 ml (5 fl oz)
    single cream
150 ml (¼ pint)
    strong coffee made
    from freshly
    ground coffee beans
4 egg yolks
100 g (4 oz) caster
    sugar
284 ml (10 fl oz)
    double cream
2 tablespoons iced
    water
Langue de Chat
    biscuits (see page
    149) to serve
    (optional)

Place the single cream and coffee in a
pan and warm gently until lukewarm.
Remove from the heat and set aside.

Whisk the egg yolks and sugar
together until the mixture is pale and
thick. Whisk in the coffee cream and
return the mixture to the pan. Heat
gently, stirring constantly, until the
custard thickens. Set aside to cool.

Whip the double cream with the
water until it forms soft peaks. Add
the coffee custard and beat lightly.
Turn into a freezerproof container.
Cover, seal and freeze until firm.

Transfer to the refrigerator
30 minutes before serving to soften.
Scoop into chilled glasses and serve
with Langue de Chat biscuits if liked.
Serves 4

COUPE GLACÉE
AUX FRAMBOISES

350 g (12 oz)
    raspberries, fresh
    or frozen
juice of 1 orange
juice of 1 lemon
175 g (6 oz)
    granulated sugar
426 ml (15 fl oz)
    double cream
3 tablespoons iced
    water
TO SERVE:
175 g (6 oz)
    raspberries
3 tablespoons kirsch
    or brandy
2 tablespoons toasted
    almonds

Rub the raspberries through a sieve or
purée in an electric blender, then sieve
to remove pips.

Mix the purée with the orange and
lemon juices and the sugar. Chill in
the refrigerator for about 1 hour.

Whip the cream with the water
until it forms soft peaks. Stir in the
raspberry purée and beat lightly
together. Turn into a rigid freezerproof container. Cover, seal and
freeze for 1 hour. Meanwhile, soak
the raspberries in the liqueur.

Remove the ice cream from the
freezer; stir, then freeze until solid.

Transfer to the refrigerator
30 minutes before serving to soften.
Spoon half the raspberries into
4 chilled glasses and scoop the ice
cream on top. Top with the
remaining raspberries and almonds.
Serves 4

VACHERIN

SWISS MERINGUE:
4 egg whites
250 g (8 oz) caster sugar
½ teaspoon vanilla essence

ITALIAN MERINGUE:
250 g (8 oz) caster sugar
150 ml (¼ pint) water
4 egg whites

FILLING:
284 ml (10 fl oz) double cream
1 tablespoon caster sugar
1 teaspoon vanilla essence
250-350 g (8-12 oz) fresh strawberries or raspberries

To make the Swiss meringue: Whisk the egg whites until stiff. Gradually whisk in the sugar and add the vanilla essence. Spoon into a piping bag fitted with a 2.5 cm (1 inch) plain nozzle. Pipe 20 fingers 10 cm (4 inches) long onto a baking sheet.

Draw an 18 to 20 cm (7 to 8 inch) circle on non-stick paper and spread with the remaining meringue. Bake the meringue fingers and circle in a preheated very cool oven, 120°C (250°F), Gas Mark ½, for 1 to 1½ hours, until crisp and pale golden. To make the Italian meringue: Heat the sugar and water gently until dissolved. Bring to the boil, and continue boiling until 120°C (250°F) is registered on a sugar thermometer.

Whisk the egg whites until stiff. Gradually pour in the hot syrup, whisking all the time; continue whisking until the meringue is cold.

Spoon into a piping bag fitted with a 2.5 cm (1 inch) star nozzle, and pipe a row of stars just inside the edge of the meringue circle. Stand the meringue fingers upright on the stars, rounded side outwards. Pipe Italian meringue between the fingers inside and outside to hold them in place. Decorate with the remaining meringue. Return to the oven for 1 hour, until the meringue base and fingers are crisp. The Italian meringue remains slightly soft and sticky. Allow to cool.

Whip the cream and sugar together until stiff and add the vanilla essence. Pile into the meringue case and top with fruit. Serve chilled.
Serves 6 to 8
NOTE: Do not fill this dessert more than 2 hours before required.

Glace au Café; Coupe Glacée aux Framboises

ORANGE GRANITA

250 g (8 oz)
  granulated sugar
600 ml (1 pint) water
300 ml (½ pint)
  unsweetened
  orange juice
2 tablespoons lemon
  juice
1 teaspoon finely
  grated orange rind

Place the sugar and water in a pan over moderate heat and stir until dissolved. Bring to the boil and boil for 5 minutes. Cool the syrup to room temperature, then stir in the orange and lemon juices and the orange rind.

Pour the mixture into a shallow freezerproof tray. Freeze to a snowy, granular texture, stirring every 30 minutes.

Spoon the granita into 4 tall glasses and serve immediately, with a straw or spoon.

Serves 4

NOTE: If the water ice freezes solid, transfer it to the refrigerator and allow to soften until it can be mashed with a fork.

Orange Granita; Amaretti Ice Cream

AMARETTI ICE CREAM

100 g (3½ oz)
  amaretti or
  macaroons (see
  page 150)
3 tablespoons
  Marsala or
  medium sherry
  (approximately)
450 ml (¾ pint)
  vanilla ice cream
TO DECORATE:
whipped cream
  (optional)
ratafia biscuits

Grind the *amaretti* or macaroons in an electric blender or crush with a rolling pin. Mix to a soft paste with the Marsala or sherry.

Spread two-thirds of the ice cream over the base and up the sides of a 600 ml (1 pint) basin. Spread the macaroon mixture in the centre and cover with the remaining ice cream, smoothing the top. Cover with foil and freeze until required.

Turn the ice cream out onto a serving dish and place in the refrigerator 30 minutes before serving to soften. Decorate with whipped cream, if using, and ratafia biscuits to serve.

Serves 4

NOTE: Avoid using soft ice cream otherwise the bombe will not hold its shape.

ZABAGLIONE

4 egg yolks
50 g (2 oz) caster
    sugar
8 tablespoons
    Marsala
sponge fingers to
    serve

Put the egg yolks and sugar in a basin and whisk until pale and foamy. Place the basin over a pan of almost boiling water, making sure the bottom of the basin does not touch the water; whisk in the Marsala. Continue whisking until the mixture expands to form a dense foamy mass that just holds its shape. Spoon into wine glasses and serve immediately, with sponge fingers.

Serves 4

CASSATA ALLA SICILIANA

3 medium eggs
75 g (3 oz) caster
    sugar
½ teaspoon finely
    grated lemon rind
½ teaspoon vanilla
    essence
scant 75 g (3 oz)
    plain flour, sifted
FILLING AND ICING:
500 g (1 lb) ricotta
    or curd cheese
125 g (4 oz) caster
    sugar
4 tablespoons
    Maraschino or
    Cointreau
50 g (2 oz) plain
    chocolate, finely
    chopped
50 g (2 oz) chopped
    mixed peel
1 tablespoon chopped
    pistachio nuts or
    almonds
TO DECORATE:
glacé cherries
sugared orange and
    lemon slices
grated chocolate

Beat the eggs, sugar, lemon rind and vanilla together, using an electric or rotary whisk, until thick enough to hold its shape. Fold in the flour.

Turn into a lined and greased 1.2 litre (2 pint) loaf tin. Cook in a preheated moderately hot oven, 190°C (375°F), Gas Mark 5, for 20 to 30 minutes, until firm. Turn onto a wire rack to cool.

Beat the cheese and sugar together until smooth and light. Add 2 tablespoons of the liqueur. Divide the mixture in half. Place one portion in the refrigerator for the icing. Mix the chocolate, peel and nuts into the other portion for the filling.

Cut the sponge horizontally into 3 layers. Place the bottom layer on a plate, sprinkle with 1 tablespoon liqueur and spread with half the filling. Cover with the middle layer, then the remaining liqueur and filling. Cover with the top sponge layer, press together and chill.

About an hour before serving, spread the icing evenly over the top and sides of the gâteau. Decorate with candied fruit and chocolate.

Serves 6

Zabaglione; Cassata alla Siciliana

ITALIAN STRAWBERRY ICE

250 g (8 oz) ripe
  strawberries
juice of ½ orange
2 teaspoons lemon
  juice
50-75 g (2-3 oz)
  icing sugar
200 ml (⅓ pint)
  whipping cream
few strawberries,
  halved, to decorate

Purée the strawberries in an electric blender or rub through a sieve, then strain. Stir in the orange and lemon juices and sweeten to taste with icing sugar. Whip the cream until thick but not stiff. Gently fold in the strawberry mixture. Turn into a freezerproof container, cover and freeze until firm.

Transfer to the refrigerator 1 hour before serving to soften. Spoon into individual glass dishes and decorate with strawberries to serve.

Serves 3 to 4

MELON WITH STRAWBERRIES

1 melon
icing sugar for dusting
350 g (12 oz) small
  strawberries,
  hulled
2 tablespoons
  Cointreau or
  Grand Marnier
juice of ½ lemon

Cut a 'lid' off the top of the melon and reserve. Scoop out the flesh with a melon baller, discarding the seeds; alternatively, cut into small cubes. Reserve the shell. Sprinkle the melon flesh with a little icing sugar, cover and chill until required. Sprinkle the strawberries with the liqueur, lemon juice and icing sugar to taste, cover and chill until required.

Just before serving, mix the melon and strawberries together, pile into the melon shell and cover with the 'lid'. Serve on a bed of crushed ice decorated with flowers and mint, if liked.

Serves 4

┌─────────── TYPES OF MELON ───────────┐

Melons are available throughout the year and the following descriptions should help you to recognise the different types when selecting for purchase.

Cantaloupe melons have sectioned mottled skins and yellow flesh. Galia melons also have a mottled surface but their flesh is green. Charentais are small green-skinned melons, with orange flesh and a sweet fragrance. The oval honeydew melons have a bright yellow skin and green flesh. Ogen melons are small with green flesh and skin.

└──────────────────────────────────────┘

ITALIAN HAZELNUT ICE

100 g (3½ oz)
  hazelnuts, toasted
  and skinned
300 ml (½ pint)
  milk
4 egg yolks
75 g (3 oz) caster
  sugar
3 drops vanilla
  essence
175 ml (6 fl oz)
  whipping cream,
  whipped

Reserve a few nuts for decoration if liked; grind the remainder coarsely.

Place the milk in a pan and bring almost to the boil. Cream together the egg yolks, sugar and vanilla essence in a bowl until pale, then gradually stir in the milk. Stir in the ground nuts.

Pour into a clean saucepan and heat gently, stirring, until the mixture is thick enough to coat the back of the spoon; do not allow to boil. Cover and leave until cold, stirring occasionally.

Fold the cream into the custard. Turn into individual freezerproof containers, cover and freeze until firm.

Transfer to the refrigerator 1 hour before serving to soften. Decorate with nuts if reserved, before serving.

Serves 4 to 5

ALMOND-STUFFED PEACHES

4 large firm peaches,
  halved and stoned
75 g (3 oz)
  macaroons, crushed
50 g (2 oz) caster
  sugar
40 g (1½ oz) butter,
  softened
1 egg yolk
½ teaspoon finely
  grated lemon rind
flaked almonds to
  decorate (optional)

Scoop a little flesh from the centre of each peach half and put in a basin. Add the macaroon crumbs, sugar, 25 g (1 oz) of the butter, the egg yolk and lemon rind and beat until smooth.

Divide between the peaches, shaping the stuffing into a mound. Top with flaked almonds if liked, and dot with the remaiing butter. Arrange in a buttered ovenproof dish.

Bake in a preheated moderate oven, 180°C (350°F), Gas Mark 4, for 25 to 35 minutes. Serve warm or cold with pouring cream.

Serves 4

Italian Almond Cookies (see page 152); Italian Strawberry Ice; Italian Hazelnut Ice

CRÊPES AUX FRAISES

125 g (4 oz) plain
  flour, sifted
pinch of salt
1 teaspoon caster sugar
1 egg
1 egg yolk
4 tablespoons milk
2 tablespoons water
2 tablespoons melted
  butter
250 g (8 oz) fresh
  strawberries, sliced
50 g (2 oz) icing
  sugar, sifted
4 tablespoons brandy
25 g (1 oz) butter

Put the flour, salt and sugar in a bowl. Make a well in the centre and add the egg and yolk. Mix well.

Gradually beat in the milk and water, stir in the melted butter and mix well. Leave for at least 2 hours.

Meanwhile mix the strawberries, icing sugar and 1 tablespoon of the brandy together. Chill for 1 hour.

Stir the batter well; if necessary add more water to give a thin batter. Lightly grease a 13-18 cm (6-7 inch) frying pan with butter and place over a moderate heat. Cook 12 crepes in the usual way (see Crêpes Suzette, opposite); keep hot.

Divide the strawberry mixture between the crepes. Fold into quarters and arrange in a buttered flambé or shallow ovenproof dish. Dot with butter and bake in a preheated moderately hot oven, 200°C (400°F), Gas Mark 6, for 10 minutes.

Warm the remaining brandy, pour over the crepes, ignite and serve.
Serves 6

BRETON CRÊPES

125 g (4 oz)
  buckwheat flour
pinch of salt
2 eggs
150 ml (¼ pint) pale
  ale
7 tablespoons water
2 teaspoons corn oil
1 tablespoon brandy
caster sugar for
  sprinkling

Sift the flour and salt into a mixing bowl and make a well in the centre. Add the eggs and half the liquid. Gradually mix in the flour to make a smooth, thick batter. Stir in the remaining liquid, corn oil and brandy. Beat for 2 to 3 minutes and leave to stand for 30 minutes. Cook the crepes as for Crêpes Suzette (opposite). As the crepes are cooked, sprinkle lightly with caster sugar and keep hot, as described.

Serve with butter, jam or honey.
Makes 14 to 16

NORMANDY APPLE CRÊPES

1 quantity crêpe
  batter (see Crêpes
  Suzette, opposite)
4 cooking apples,
  peeled and cut into
  thin wedges
75-125 g (3-4 oz)
  butter
125 g (4 oz) soft
  light brown sugar
ground cinnamon for
  sprinkling

Make and cook the crepes as for Crêpes Suzette. Lay the crepes flat on baking sheets and arrange the apple on top, leaving a border of about 1 cm (½ inch). Dot with the butter and sprinkle liberally with the sugar and cinnamon to taste.

Place in a preheated moderate oven, 180°C (350°F), Gas Mark 4, for about 30 minutes, until the apples are just soft but hold their shape. Serve hot.
Serves 4 or 8

TO STORE PANCAKES AND CRÊPES

Leftover batter can be stored in a covered container in the refrigerator for up to three days. It is a very good idea to keep a ready supply of pancakes so that you can produce delicious desserts in an instant, such as those suggested here.

Use any one of the batters given here and make up in various sized crepes. Cool the crepes on a wire rack. When cold, stack, separated by rounds of greased greaseproof paper or clingfilm. Pack closely in quantities of 8 to 12 in foil or a polythene bag. Store in a refrigerator for up to five days or in a freezer for up to four months.

Thaw frozen pancakes or crepes, still wrapped, at room temperature for about 2 hours or in a refrigerator overnight.

Crêpes aux Fraises

CRÊPES SUZETTE

BATTER:
125 g (4 oz) plain flour
pinch of salt
1 egg, beaten
300 ml (½ pint) milk
1 tablespoon oil
ORANGE SAUCE:
50 g (2 oz) butter
50 g (2 oz) caster sugar
grated rind and juice of 2 oranges
2 tablespoons Grand Marnier
2 tablespoons brandy

Sift the flour and salt into a bowl and make a well in the centre. Add the egg, then gradually add half the milk, stirring constantly. Add the oil and beat until smooth. Add remaining milk and leave to stand for 30 minutes.

To cook the pancakes, heat a 15 cm (6 inch) omelet pan and add a few drops of oil. Pour in 1 tablespoon of batter and tilt the pan to coat the bottom evenly. Cook until the underside is brown, then turn over and cook for 10 seconds. Turn out onto a wire rack and cover with a tea towel. Repeat with the remaining batter, stacking the cooked pancakes one on top of the other.

To make the orange sauce: Melt the butter in a frying pan, add the sugar, orange rind and juice and heat until bubbling. Dip each crêpe into the sauce, fold into quarters then place in a warmed serving dish.

Add the Grand Marnier and brandy to the pan, heat gently, then ignite. Pour the flaming liquid over the crêpes and serve immediately
Serves 4

CRÊPES AU CHOCOLAT

BATTER:
125 g (4 oz) plain flour
pinch of salt
2 tablespoons caster sugar
1 tablespoon instant coffee powder
1 tablespoon cocoa powder
2 eggs, beaten
250 ml (8 fl oz) milk
1 tablespoon oil
SAUCE:
175 g (6 oz) plain chocolate, chopped
150 ml (¼ pint) water
1 teaspoon instant coffee powder
125 g (4 oz) sugar
FILLING:
284 ml (10 fl oz) double cream
2 tablespoons rum

Make and cook the pancakes as for Crêpes Suzette (see left), sifting the sugar, coffee and cocoa with the flour and salt; set aside to cool.

To make the sauce: Place the chocolate, 2 tablespoons of the water and the coffee in a small pan and heat gently until melted. Add the remaining water and the sugar and heat gently, stirring, until dissolved, then simmer, uncovered, for 10 minutes. Leave to cool.

To make the filling: Whip the cream until fairly stiff. Fold in the rum.

Place a spoonful of cream on each pancake, roll up and place on a serving dish. Just before serving, pour over a little chocolate sauce. Serve the remaining sauce separately.
Serves 6

Crêpes Suzette; Crêpes au Chocolat

PROFITEROLES AU CARAMEL

CHOUX PASTRY:
150 ml (¼ pint)
   water
50 g (2 oz) butter
65 g (2½ oz) plain
   flour
pinch of salt
2 eggs, lightly beaten
FILLING:
250 ml (8 fl oz)
   double cream,
   lightly whipped
CARAMEL SAUCE:
75 g (3 oz)
   granulated sugar
4 tablespoons cold
   water
142 ml (5 fl oz)
   double cream

Put the water and butter in a pan and bring to the boil. Take off the heat, add the flour and salt and beat until the paste is smooth and forms a ball. Cool slightly, then gradually beat in the eggs, to form a smooth shiny paste.

Spoon into a piping bag fitted with a 2.5 cm (1 inch) plain nozzle and pipe small mounds on greased baking sheets. Bake in a preheated moderately hot oven, 200°C (400°F), Gas Mark 6, for 15 to 20 minutes, until risen and golden.

Transfer to a wire rack and split each one. Cool, then fill with cream.

Heat the sugar in a pan over low heat until dissolved. Increase the heat and cook to a golden brown caramel. Remove from the heat and carefully add the water. Return to the heat and stir until the caramel dissolves. Cool, then whip into the cream.

Arrange the profiteroles on a dish and spoon over the sauce. Serve chilled.
Serves 6

SOUFFLÉ PRALINE

1 tablespoon plain
   flour
150 ml (¼ pint)
   milk
50 g (2 oz) caster
   sugar
few drops vanilla
   essence
4 eggs, separated
25 g (1 oz) butter,
   softened
PRALINE:
40 g (1½ oz)
   almonds, chopped
40 g (1½ oz)
   hazelnuts,
   chopped
75 g (3 oz)
   granulated sugar
2 tablespoons water

To make the praline: Put the nuts on a baking sheet and place under a preheated moderate grill until lightly browned; cool. Put the sugar and water in a small pan and boil until the sugar caramelizes. Stir in the nuts and pour immediately onto an oiled baking sheet. Leave until cold, then pound to a coarse powder in a mortar.

Beat the flour with 2 tablespoons of the milk in a pan until smooth. Add the remaining milk, sugar and vanilla essence. Slowly bring to the boil, stirring. Cook for 1 minute.

Beat in the egg yolks, one at a time. Stir in the butter. Cool, then stir in the praline. Whisk the egg whites until stiff and fold into the mixture.

Turn into a 1.2-1.5 litre (2-2½ pint) buttered soufflé dish. Cook in a preheated moderately hot oven, 190°C (375°F), Gas Mark 5, for 35 to 40 minutes, until risen and golden. Serve immediately.
Serves 4 to 6

CRÈME PÂTISSIÈRE

50 g (2 oz) caster
   sugar
3 egg yolks
2 tablespoons plain
   flour
2 tablespoons
   cornflour
300 ml (½ pint)
   milk
few drops of vanilla
   essence

Whisk together the sugar and egg yolks until pale and light. Sift together the flour and cornflour and gradually whisk into the egg mixture.

Boil the milk, then pour onto the egg mixture, whisking constantly. Transfer to a pan and heat, stirring constantly, until thickened. Beat in the vanilla essence and leave to cool.

Use as a filling for cakes and sweet pastries, such as choux buns (see left) and Cherry and Almond Tart (see page 97).
Makes 450 ml (¾ pint)

LEFT: *Profiteroles au Caramel*
OPPOSITE: *French Baked Apples*

FRENCH BAKED APPLES

250 g (8 oz) plain
    flour
pinch of salt
125 g (4 oz) butter
1 tablespoon caster
    sugar
3-5 tablespoons iced
    water
4 large dessert apples,
    peeled and cored
4 tablespoons quince
    or plum jam
beaten egg to glaze

Sift the flour and salt into a bowl.
Rub in the butter until the mixture
resembles fine breadcrumbs, then stir
in the sugar. Mix in enough water to
give a smooth, pliable dough.

Divide the dough into 4 pieces and
roll each into a square. Fill the centres
of the apples with the jam and place
on the squares.

Brush the edges of the squares with
water and wrap the pastry around the
apples. Trim any excess pastry and
press the edges firmly to seal.
Decorate with pastry leaves cut from
the trimmings.

Place on a baking sheet and brush
with beaten egg. Bake in a preheated
moderate oven, 160°C (325°F), Gas
Mark 3, for 20 to 25 minutes until
golden. Serve hot, with cream.
Serves 4

STRAWBERRY MILLE FEUILLE

1 × 368 g (13 oz)
    packet frozen puff
    pastry, thawed
500 g (1 lb)
    strawberries
284 ml (10 fl oz)
    double cream,
    whipped
1 tablespoon icing
    sugar, sifted
4 tablespoons
    redcurrant jelly
2 teaspoons water

Divide the pastry into 3 equal pieces
and roll each into a rectangle, about
15 × 35 cm (6 × 14 inches). Place on
dampened baking sheets, prick well
all over and chill for 15 minutes.

Bake in a preheated hot oven,
220°C (425°F), Gas Mark 7, for 12 to
15 minutes until golden. Turn the
pastry over and bake for 5 minutes.

Cool on a wire rack. Trim the
edges to neaten.

Slice half the strawberries; halve
the remainder and set aside. Fold the
sliced strawberries into the cream
with the icing sugar. Spread half the
mixture onto one piece of the pastry.
Place a second layer of pastry on top,
spread with the remaining mixture
and cover with the last piece of
pastry.

Heat the redcurrant jelly with the
water. Brush the top of the pastry
with this glaze and arrange the
remaining strawberries on top. Brush
with glaze.
Serves 8

AUSTRIAN CURD CAKE

75 g (3 oz) butter
175 g (6 oz)
    digestive biscuits,
    crushed
50 g (2 oz) demerara
    sugar
350 g (12 oz) curd
    cheese
50 g (2 oz) caster
    sugar
3 eggs, separated
grated rind of 1 lemon
15 g (½ oz) gelatine,
    soaked in 3
    tablespoons water
426 ml (15 fl oz)
    whipping cream,
    whipped

Melt the butter in a pan; mix in the
biscuit crumbs and demerara sugar.
Spread half the mixture over the base
of a 20 cm (8 inch) loose-bottomed
cake tin and chill in the refrigerator.

Meanwhile, place the cheese in a
bowl and beat in the sugar, egg yolks
and lemon rind. Stir the soaked
gelatine in a bowl over a pan of hot
water until dissolved, then stir into
the cheese mixture.

Fold two-thirds of the cream into
the cheese mixture. Whisk the egg
whites until stiff and fold into the
mixture. Spoon over the biscuit base
and place in the refrigerator for
10 minutes. Spread the remaining
crumbs over the top and chill in the
refrigerator for 2 hours.

Remove from the tin and decorate
with piped cream.
Serves 8

APPLE STRUDEL

PASTRY:
175 g (6 oz) strong
  plain flour
¼ teaspoon salt
1 egg (size 2)
4 tablespoons
  lukewarm water
1 tablespoon oil
melted butter for
  brushing,
  approximately
  50 g (2 oz)
FILLING:
6 large cooking
  apples, peeled,
  cored and thinly
  sliced
125 g (4 oz) caster
  sugar
1½ teaspoons ground
  cinnamon
75 g (3 oz) sultanas
2 teaspoons grated
  lemon rind
50 g (2 oz) fresh
  breadcrumbs, fried
  in butter

Sift the flour and salt into a bowl. Beat the egg until frothy, stir in the water and oil and add to the flour. Mix until smooth, then turn onto a lightly floured surface. Knead for 15 minutes, until the dough is elastic..Cover and leave for 20 minutes.

Mix the apples, sugar, cinnamon, sultanas and lemon rind together for the filling. Brush the dough with melted butter and roll out to 3 mm (⅛ inch) thickness on a floured cloth, then stretch the dough using both hands until it is paper thin. If dry patches appear, brush with melted butter; if the pastry tears, pinch it together. Brush generously with melted butter and trim edges.

Sprinkle the pastry with the fried breadcrumbs and spoon the apple mixture in a 7.5 cm (3 inch) band along one side, to within 5 cm (2 inches) of the edges. Fold the pastry over the filling and roll up, from the filling side, by lifting the cloth.

Lift the strudel onto a greased baking sheet, curving it into a horseshoe shape if necessary. Brush with melted butter. Bake in a preheated hot oven, 230°C (450°F), Gas Mark 8, for 10 minutes. Lower the heat to 200°C (400°F), Gas Mark 6, and bake for a further 20 minutes or until the strudel is crisp and brown, basting frequently with melted butter. Serve warm.
Serves 10 to 12

BABAS AU RHUM

15 g (½ oz) dried
  yeast
2 tablespoons
  lukewarm water
pinch of caster sugar
250 g (8 oz) strong
  plain flour
1 tablespoon sugar
3 eggs
½ teaspoon salt
75 g (3 oz) currants
6 tablespoons rum
100 g (3½ oz)
  butter, softened
250 g (8 oz)
  granulated sugar
scant 900 ml
  (1½ pints) water
250 g (8 oz) fresh
  strawberries,
  raspberries or
  cherries to serve

Mix the yeast with the water and caster sugar and leave for about 10 minutes until frothy.

Put the flour and sugar in a bowl and make a well in the centre. Add the yeast mixture. Break in the eggs and add the salt. Work to a smooth, elastic dough. Cover and leave in a warm place until doubled in bulk. Meanwhile, soak the currants in 2 tablespoons of the rum.

Knead the butter and currants into the dough. Spoon into 8 small greased baba tins, cover and leave in a warm place for 45 to 50 minutes, until the dough has risen to 5 mm (¼ inch) below the top of the tins. Bake in a preheated moderately hot oven, 200°C (400°F), Gas Mark 6, for 15 to 20 minutes, until golden; cool.

Heat the granulated sugar and water in a pan until dissolved, then boil for 3 to 4 minutes until slightly thickened and clear. Stir in the remaining rum and spoon over the babas. Fill with fruit to serve.
Makes 8

LINZER TORTEN

125 g (4 oz) butter
175 g (6 oz) icing
  sugar, sifted
1 egg, beaten
finely grated rind of
  1 lemon
125 g (4 oz) ground
  almonds
125 g (4 oz) plain
  flour, sifted
FILLING:
5 tablespoons
  raspberry conserve
TO FINISH:
2 tablespoons apricot
  jam, boiled and
  sieved

Cream the butter and icing sugar until fluffy; beat in egg and lemon rind. Fold in the nuts and flour. Wrap in cling film and chill for 1 hour.

Carefully roll out the dough on a floured surface to a thin round and use to line a 23 cm (9 inch) flan tin. Spread with conserve, leaving a 2.5 cm (1 inch) border. Roll out trimmings and cut into strips to form a lattice across the flan. Shape remaining dough into a rope to fit around the edge; flatten with a fork.

Bake in a preheated moderately hot oven, 190°C (375°F), Gas Mark 5, for 30 minutes. Cool, then brush with jam.
Makes one 23 cm (9 inch) tart

Babas au Rhum

TARTE FRANÇAISE

1 × 368 g (13 oz)
 packet frozen puff
 pastry, thawed
1 egg yolk, mixed
 with 1 teaspoon
 water
GLAZE:
4 tablespoons apricot
 jam
2 tablespoons water
1 teaspoon lemon
 juice
FILLING:
125 g (4 oz) black
 grapes, seeded
125 g (4 oz) green
 grapes, seeded
125 g (4 oz)
 strawberries

Roll out the pastry to a rectangle, about 30 × 20 cm (12 × 8 inches). Sprinkle the pastry lightly with flour and fold in half lengthways.

Cut out a rectangle from the folded edge, leaving a 3.5 cm (1½ inch) wide band on the remaining 3 sides.

Open out the rectangle and roll out until 30 × 20 cm (12 × 8 inches). Place on a dampened baking sheet, prick the pastry all over and dampen the edges.

Open out the band of pastry and place on the rectangle to make a border. Knock up the edges and mark a pattern on the border with a knife. Brush the border with the egg yolk and water mixture and bake in a preheated hot oven, 220°C (425°F), Gas Mark 7, for 20 to 25 minutes until golden brown.

Heat the jam with the water and lemon juice then sieve and reheat. Use to brush the base of the pastry case, then arrange the fruit in rows down the tart. Brush generously with the glaze. Serve cold.
Serves 6

French Apple Flan

FRENCH APPLE FLAN

PÂTE SUCRÉE:
175 g (6 oz) plain
 flour
75 g (3 oz) butter
75 g (3 oz) caster
 sugar
3 egg yolks
few drops of vanilla
 essence
FILLING:
1.5 kg (3 lb) cooking
 apples, peeled,
 cored and thinly
 sliced
50 g (2 oz) caster
 sugar
GLAZE:
4 tablespoons apricot
 jam
juice of ½ lemon

Sift the flour onto a marble slab or cool work surface. Make a well in the centre and in it place the butter, sugar, egg yolks and essence. Using the fingertips of one hand, work these ingredients together, then draw in the flour. Knead lightly until smooth and chill for 1 hour.

Roll out the pastry very thinly and use to line a 25 cm (10 inch) fluted flan ring. Fill the case generously with apples, then arrange an overlapping layer of apples on top. Sprinkle with the sugar. Bake in a preheated moderately hot oven, 190°C (375°F), Gas Mark 5, for 35 to 40 minutes.

Meanwhile, heat the jam with the lemon juice, then strain and brush over the apples. Serve hot or cold, with cream.
Serves 8

FREEZING APPLE SLICES

Although apples are on sale all year round, it is a good idea to freeze them in September and October when there is a glut, to have some sliced apples on hand for making desserts.

Choose apples which have no bruises, blemishes or signs of decay. Both dessert and cooking apples can be prepared in the following way; however, prepare the fruit in small batches to prevent discoloration. Peel and core the apples, then cut them into slices. Immediately place in a bowl containing iced water and lemon juice. Dessert apples do not need blanching. Blanch cooking apples in boiling water for 1 minute, drain and cool quickly in iced water, then drain again and pat dry with kitchen paper.

Pack in rigid containers, sprinkling each layer with sugar, and allowing 125 g (4 oz) sugar to each 500 g (1 lb) fruit. Seal, label and freeze for up to 12 months.

To thaw, leave to stand in container at room temperature for 1 to 2 hours. To use in dessert recipes reduce the amount of sugar in the recipe to taste.

ITALIAN CURD TART

FLAN PASTRY:
250 g (8 oz) plain flour, sifted
75 g (3 oz) caster sugar
125 g (4 oz) butter, softened
1 teaspoon finely grated lemon rind
2 egg yolks

CURD FILLING:
350 g (12 oz) ricotta or curd cheese, sieved
75 g (3 oz) caster sugar
3 eggs, beaten
1 teaspoon each grated lemon and orange rind
75 g (3 oz) candied peel, chopped
50 g (2 oz) blanched almonds, chopped

TO DECORATE:
icing sugar

Mix together the flour and sugar in a bowl, make a well in the centre and add the butter, lemon rind and egg yolks. Gradually draw the flour into the centre, using the fingertips, and work the ingredients to a firm, smooth dough. Cover and chill for 1 hour.

Meanwhile, prepare the filling. Mix the cheese and sugar together in a basin. Gradually beat in the eggs, then add the remaining ingredients. Mix well.

Roll out the pastry and use to line an 18 to 20 cm (7 to 8 inch) flan ring standing on a baking sheet. Spread the filling evenly in the flan case.

Bake in a preheated moderate oven, 180°C (350°F), Gas Mark 4, for 45 to 50 minutes. Cool slightly, then transfer to a wire rack and leave until cold. Sprinkle with icing sugar to serve.

Serves 6 to 8

NOTE: If preferred, decorate the tart with a lattice pattern of pastry strips, before baking.

GÂTEAU DE NOISETTES AUX FRUITS

PASTRY:
150 g (5 oz) plain flour
pinch of salt
250 g (8 oz) hazelnuts, ground
125 g (4 oz) caster sugar
125 g (4 oz) butter, softened
1 egg yolk

FILLING:
284 ml (10 fl oz) double cream, whipped
1 fresh pineapple, peeled, cored and sliced

Sift the flour and salt onto a board, make a well in the centre and put in the hazelnuts, sugar, butter and egg yolk. Work the flour into the centre, using the fingers; mix to a smooth paste. Cover and chill for 1 hour.

Divide the dough into 3 pieces. Roll out each piece and use to line the bases of three 20 cm (8 inch) flan rings, placed on baking sheets. Prick with a fork. Mark one round into 8 triangles. Bake in a preheated moderately hot oven, 190°C (375°F), Gas Mark 5, for 10 minutes or until golden brown. Break the marked round into triangles. Cool.

Put one circle on a serving dish and spread with a layer of cream. Top with half the pineapple, cover with the other round and spread with cream.

Decorate with the remaining cream: pipe 8 lines radiating from the centre, place the pastry triangles on these and top with the remaining pineapple. Finish with cream rosettes.

Serves 8

PETITS POTS AU CAFÉ

25 g (1 oz) butter
2 tablespoons caster sugar
1 tablespoon rum
2 teaspoons instant coffee powder
3 eggs, separated

TO DECORATE:
120 ml (4 fl oz) double cream, whipped
few walnut halves

Put the butter, sugar, rum and coffee in a bowl over a pan of hot water and stir until melted. Add the egg yolks and mix well. Leave to cook over the hot water for 5 minutes, stirring occasionally. Remove from the heat and cool.

Whisk the egg whites until stiff, then fold into the coffee mixture. Spoon into individual ramekins and decorate each with piped cream and walnuts.

Serves 4

Gâteau de Noisettes aux Fruits

SORBET AUX PÊCHES

500 g (1 lb) ripe
  peaches, skinned
  and stoned
2 ripe apricots,
  skinned and stoned
175 g (6 oz) caster
  sugar
juice of 1/2 lemon
6 tablespoons cold
  water
fresh peach slices to
  decorate

Work the fruit in an electric blender or rub through a sieve until smooth.

Put the sugar, lemon juice and water in a pan and heat, stirring, until dissolved. Bring to the boil and simmer for 2 minutes. Cool, then stir into the purée.

Turn into a freezerproof container and freeze for about 1 hour, until small ice crystals have formed around the edge. Whisk thoroughly, then return to the container and freeze for at least 6 to 8 hours.

Transfer to the refrigerator about 1 hour before serving, to soften slightly. Spoon into serving dishes and top with peach slices. Serve with boudoir biscuits.
Serves 4

OMELETTE SOUFFLÉ AU GRAND MARNIER

6 macaroons
4 tablespoons Grand
  Marnier
100 g (3½ oz) caster
  sugar
few drops vanilla
  essence
5 eggs, separated

Carefully dip the macaroons into the liqueur. Arrange in the base of a gratin dish. Sprinkle over any remaining Grand Marnier and 1 tablespoon sugar.

Beat the egg yolks, remaining sugar and vanilla essence until thick and creamy. Whisk the egg whites until stiff and fold into the yolk mixture. Spoon over the macaroons, and shape into a dome.

Make shallow slits over the surface to enable the heat to penetrate. Bake in a preheated moderately hot oven, 190°C (375°F), Gas Mark 5, for 20 minutes, until well risen and golden brown. Serve immediately.
Serves 6

TARTELETTES AUX FRUITS

PASTRY:
175 g (6 oz) plain
  flour
pinch of salt
65 g (2½ oz) caster
  sugar
3 egg yolks
100 g (3½ oz)
  butter, softened
FILLING:
4 tablespoons
  redcurrant jelly
1 tablespoon water
350-500 g (12 oz-
  1 lb) prepared fresh
  fruit (e.g.
  strawberries,
  raspberries,
  grapes, cherries,
  apricots,
  tangerines)

Sift the flour onto a pastry board and make a well in the centre. Put the salt, sugar and egg yolks into the well and gradually work into the flour until smooth. Quickly knead in the butter. Form into a ball, cover and chill for 1 hour.

Roll out the pastry and use to line eight 7.5 cm (3 inch) tartlet tins; chill for 20 minutes. Bake blind in a preheated moderately hot oven, 200°C (400°F), Gas Mark 6, for 10 to 12 minutes, until the pastry is golden brown; cool.

Stir the redcurrant jelly with the water in a pan over low heat until blended. Brush the bases of the pastry cases with this glaze. Arrange the fruit on top as desired and brush with glaze. Serve with cream.
Makes 8

GÂTEAU AUX FRAISES

3 eggs, separated
125 g (4 oz) caster
  sugar
grated rind and juice
  of 1/2 lemon
50 g (2 oz) semolina
25 g (1 oz) ground
  almonds
TO FINISH:
284 ml (10 fl oz)
  double cream,
  whipped
250 g (8 oz)
  strawberries,
  halved
4 tablespoons
  redcurrant jelly
2 teaspoons water
50 g (2 oz) almonds,
  chopped and
  browned

Cream the egg yolks with the sugar, lemon rind and juice until thick. Stir in the semolina and ground almonds, then fold in the stiffly whisked egg whites. Turn the mixture into a lined, greased and floured 23 cm (9 inch) moule a manqué tin and bake in a preheated moderate oven, 180°C (350°F), Gas Mark 4, for 35 to 40 minutes. Turn onto a wire rack to cool.

Split the cake in half and sandwich together with three-quarters of the cream. Arrange the strawberries on the top.

Heat the redcurrant jelly with the water, sieve, reheat and use to glaze the strawberries and side of the cake. Press the browned almonds around the side and pipe the remaining cream around the top to decorate.
Makes one 23 cm (9 inch) gâteau

*Omelette Soufflé au Grand Marnier; Tartelettes aux Fruits;
Sorbet aux Pêches*

WAFERS, BISCUITS AND SAUCES

Many of the desserts in this exciting collection taste that much better served with an accompanying sauce, or with home-made biscuits or wafers. Sponge puddings and ice creams are enhanced by appropriate sauces. Choose from chocolate, Melba, butterscotch, apricot, and fudge-flavoured sauces (see page 153), according to the dessert. Vanilla Cream Sauce (page 153) is a delicious, creamy sauce which can be served with puddings and pies in place of custard or cream. It is certainly superior to the usual 'mock' custard, made with custard powder.

Crisp wafers and biscuits, such as Brandy Snaps (page 148), Cigarettes Russes (page 149) and Almond Curls (page 151) are ideal to serve with ices, sorbets, whips, fools and mousses. They provide a crisp contrast to these smooth-textured desserts. The attractive Lace Baskets (page 148) make effective serving 'dishes' for whips, syllabub and ices. Serve these at dinner parties and your guests will undoubtedly be impressed.

Making these biscuits and wafers is fun too! Most of the mixtures are quick to prepare and cook. The time-consuming task is shaping them after baking – but this is also the enjoyable part. For brandy snaps and cigarettes russes you will need quite a few wooden spoons; for the lace baskets you will need a number of upturned glasses to create the basket shapes. All of these biscuits and wafers can be prepared in advance and stored in an airtight tin for several days.

BRANDY SNAPS

125 g (4 oz) butter
125 g (4 oz)
  demerara sugar
125 g (4 oz) golden
  syrup
125 g (4 oz) plain
  flour
1 teaspoon ground
  ginger

Put the butter, sugar and syrup in a saucepan and heat gently until the butter has melted and the sugar dissolved. Cool slightly, then sift in the flour and ginger. Beat well.

Place teaspoonfuls of the mixture 10 cm (4 inches) apart on baking sheets. Bake in a preheated moderate oven, 180°C (350°F), Gas Mark 4, for 10 to 12 minutes, until golden.

Leave to cool slightly, then remove with a palette knife and roll around the handle of a wooden spoon. Leave for 1 to 2 minutes to set, then slip off carefully onto a wire rack to cool.
Makes 35
NOTE: If the mixture cools and becomes too thick, spread it out thinly with a palette knife to flatten.

If the biscuits become too brittle to roll, return them to the oven for 30 seconds to soften.

Lace Baskets

NUTTY CURLS

75 g (3 oz) butter or
  margarine
75 g (3 oz) caster
  sugar
50 g (2 oz) plain
  flour
50 g (2 oz)
  hazelnuts,
  chopped

Cream the butter or margarine and sugar together until light and fluffy. Stir in the flour and hazelnuts and mix well. Place small teaspoonfuls of the mixture well apart on greased baking sheets and flatten with a damp fork.

Bake in a preheated moderately hot oven, 190°C (375°F), Gas Mark 5, for 6 to 8 minutes, until pale golden.

Leave on the baking sheets for 1 minute, then remove with a palette knife and lay on rolling pins to curl. Leave until set then remove carefully.
Makes 25

LACE BASKETS

50 g (2 oz) butter or
  margarine
50 g (2 oz) demerara
  sugar
50 g (2 oz) golden
  syrup
50 g (2 oz) plain
  flour, sifted

Place the butter or margarine, sugar and syrup in a pan and heat gently until the fat has melted and the sugar dissolved. Cool slightly then beat in the flour.

Place 12 heaped teaspoonfuls of the mixture at least 10 cm (4 inches) apart on 3 baking sheets. Bake in a preheated moderate oven, 180°C (350°F), Gas Mark 4, for 10 to 12 minutes, until golden.

Leave to cool slightly, then remove with a palette knife. Mould over the base of an inverted glass, with the top side of the biscuit touching the glass. Leave to set then remove carefully.
Makes 12
NOTE: If the mixture cools and becomes too thick, spread it out thinly with a palette knife to flatten.

Do not bake more than 4 at a time or they will set before you have time to mould them. If they become too brittle to handle, return them to the oven for 30 seconds to soften.

LANGUE DE CHAT
BISCUITS

50 g (2 oz) butter
50 g (2 oz) caster
 sugar
2 egg whites
50 g (2 oz) plain
 flour, sifted
few drops of vanilla
 essence

Cream the butter and sugar together until light and fluffy. Whisk the egg whites lightly and gradually beat into the creamed mixture with the flour and vanilla essence.

Place in a piping bag fitted with a 1 cm (⅜ inch) plain nozzle and pipe 7.5 cm (3 inch) lengths on greased and floured baking sheets; alternatively, pipe into rounds.

Bake in a preheated moderately hot oven, 200°C (400°F), Gas Mark 6, for 10 minutes; the biscuits should be pale golden, but darker around the edges. Transfer to a wire rack to cool.
Makes 20 to 24

CIGARETTES RUSSES

1 egg white
50 g (2 oz) caster
 sugar
25 g (1 oz) butter,
 melted
15 g (½ oz) plain
 flour
¼ teaspoon vanilla
 essence

Place the egg white in a bowl. Add the sugar and beat until smooth. Add remaining ingredients and beat well.

Spread the mixture thinly into 10 × 6 cm (4 × 2½ inch) oblongs on greased and floured baking sheets. Bake in a preheated moderately hot oven, 200°C (400°F), Gas Mark 6, for 4 to 5 minutes, until golden.

Leave on the baking sheets for 30 seconds, then scrape off with a palette knife and place top side down on a table top. Roll each tightly around a small wooden spoon handle or pencil and hold firmly for a few seconds. Slide off and allow to cool.
Makes 15
NOTE: Do not bake more than 3 at a time or they will set before you have time to shape them.

Brandy Snaps; Cigarettes Russes

MACAROONS

250 g (8 oz) caster
  sugar
150 g (5 oz) ground
  almonds
1 tablespoon rice flour
2 egg whites
rice paper
25 split almonds

Mix the sugar, almonds and rice flour together and set aside. Beat the egg whites lightly, add the dry ingredients, and beat to a smooth, firm consistency.

Leave to stand for 5 minutes then roll into small balls and place slightly apart on a baking sheet lined with rice paper. Flatten slightly and place a split almond on each one.

Bake in a preheated moderate oven, 180°C (350°F), Gas Mark 4, for 20 minutes. Cool on the baking sheet.
Makes 25

ALMOND GALETTES

125 g (4 oz) butter or
  margarine
50 g (2 oz) caster
  sugar
1 egg yolk
50 g (2 oz) ground
  almonds
175 g (6 oz) plain
  flour
TOPPING:
125 g (4 oz) icing
  sugar, sifted
1 egg white
50 g (2 oz) almonds,
  shredded

Cream the butter or margarine and sugar together, then add the egg yolk and beat well. Add the ground almonds and flour and mix well. Knead lightly and roll out thinly. Cut into rounds using a 6 cm (2½ inch) plain cutter and place on a greased baking sheet.

For the topping, mix the icing sugar with the egg white, then add the shredded almonds and stir well. Spoon over the biscuits and bake in a preheated moderate oven, 180°C (350°F), Gas Mark 4, for 15 to 20 minutes, until golden brown. Cool on the baking sheet.
Makes 24

Macaroons; Almond Galettes

SPONGE FINGERS

Speed and gentleness are essential, as this very light mixture quickly loses its volume if handled heavily or left to stand. Have all ingredients at room temperature.

50 g (2 oz) caster
    sugar
2 eggs
few drops of vanilla
    essence
50 g (2 oz) plain
    flour, sifted
caster sugar for
    dredging

Whisk the sugar, eggs and vanilla essence in a mixing bowl over a pan of hot water until thick. (If using an electric beater, the hot water is unnecessary.)

Place the mixture in a piping bag fitted with a 1 cm (½ inch) plain nozzle and pipe into finger lengths on greased and floured baking sheets. Dust well with caster sugar and bake in a preheated moderately hot oven, 190°C (375°F), Gas Mark 5, for 6 to 8 minutes until golden brown. Transfer to a wire rack to cool.
Makes 22

Variation: To make Sponge Drops instead of Fingers, place the mixture in a piping bag fitted with a 1 cm (½ inch) plain nozzle. Pipe into discs, 3.5 cm (1½ inches) in diameter, onto greased and floured baking sheets.

Bake as for Sponge Fingers. There should be enough for about 20 to 24.

ALMOND CURLS

75 g (3 oz) butter
75 g (3 oz) caster
    sugar
50 g (2 oz) plain
    flour, sifted
75 g (3 oz) flaked
    almonds

Cream the butter and sugar together until light and fluffy. Stir in the flour and almonds and mix well. Place teaspoonfuls of the mixture well apart on greased baking sheets and flatten with a damp fork.

Bake in a preheated moderately hot oven, 200°C (400°F), Gas Mark 6, for 6 to 8 minutes until pale golden. Leave on the baking sheets for 1 minute, then remove with a palette knife and place on rolling pins to curl. Leave until set in a curl, then remove very carefully.
Makes 25

Sponge Fingers; Almond Curls

┌─────────────────────────────────────┐
│ SERVING BISCUITS AND SAUCES

The crisp biscuits and wafers in this chapter are ideal to serve with ices and light desserts. Refer to the chapters on Ices and Sorbets, and Soufflés, Mousses and Light Desserts, for serving suggestions.

Nutty Curls are delicious served with soft fruit desserts such as Raspberry Chantilly (see page 12). Brandy Snaps go well with Oranges in Caramel (see page 23). Sponge Fingers are the traditional accompaniment for Zabaglione (see page 133).

The sauces in this chapter make delicious ice cream toppings – try different combinations of ices and sauces for yourself.
└─────────────────────────────────────┘

Tuiles d'Oranges

TUILES D'ORANGES

1 egg white
50 g (2 oz) caster
  sugar
25 g (1 oz) plain
  flour
grated rind of
  ½ orange
25 g (1 oz) butter,
  melted

Place the egg white in a bowl and beat in the sugar. Add the remaining ingredients and mix well.

Place teaspoonfuls of the mixture well apart on greased baking sheets and spread out thinly with a palette knife.

Bake in a preheated moderately hot oven, 190°C (375°F), Gas Mark 5, for 6 to 8 minutes, until pale golden brown.

Leave on the baking sheets for a few seconds, then remove with a palette knife and place on a rolling pin to curl. Leave until cool then remove carefully.

Makes about 15

NOTE: Do not bake more than 4 at a time or they will set before you have time to shape them.

ITALIAN ALMOND COOKIES

125 g (4 oz) butter,
  softened
200 g (7 oz) caster
  sugar
1 size 5 egg, beaten
4 drops almond
  essence
250 g (8 oz) plain
  flour
1 teaspoon baking
  powder
1 tablespoon milk
  (approximately)
50 g (2 oz) blanched
  almonds, finely
  chopped
2 tablespoons apricot
  jam

Cream the butter and sugar together until light and fluffy, then beat in the egg and almond essence. Sift the flour and baking powder together and stir into the mixture with enough milk to form a smooth paste.

Roll teaspoonfuls of the mixture into balls. Roll in chopped almonds and place well apart on a greased baking sheet. Make a deep dent in the centre of each and fill with jam.

Bake in a preheated moderately hot oven, 200°C (400°F), Gas Mark 6, for 12 to 15 minutes, until golden. Leave for 5 minutes then transfer to a wire rack to cool. Store in an airtight tin.

Makes about 36

(Illustrated on page 134)

APRICOT SAUCE

125 g (4 oz) dried
  apricots, soaked
  overnight in
  600 ml
  (1 pint) water
50 g (2 oz) caster
  sugar
2 teaspoons lemon
  juice

Place the apricots and their soaking liquid in a pan, cover and simmer for 15 minutes. Add the sugar and lemon juice, stirring until the sugar has dissolved. Sieve or work in an electric blender or food processor until smooth. Serve hot or cold with vanilla ice cream.

Makes 450 ml (¾ pint)

MINCEMEAT SAUCE

2 dessert apples,
  peeled, cored and
  finely chopped
3 tablespoons water
250 g (8 oz)
  mincemeat (see
  page 99)
grated rind and juice
  of 1 orange
2 tablespoons brandy
  (optional)

Place the apples in a pan with the water. Cover and simmer gently for 5 minutes. Stir in the mincemeat, orange rind and juice and heat through. Stir in the brandy, if using. Serve warm, with vanilla ice cream.

Makes 450 ml (¾ pint)

CHOCOLATE SAUCE

175 g (6 oz) plain chocolate, chopped
250 ml (8 fl oz) milk
1 teaspoon instant coffee granules
50 g (2 oz) soft brown sugar

Place all the ingredients in a small pan and heat gently until melted. Stir well and simmer, uncovered, for 2 to 3 minutes. Serve warm or cold, with vanilla, coffee or chocolate ice cream, or profiteroles.
Makes 450 ml (¾ pint)

MELBA SAUCE

350 g (12 oz) raspberries
50 g (2 oz) icing sugar, sifted

Place the raspberries and icing sugar in a blender or food processor. Blend to a purée, then sieve to remove the pips. Serve with vanilla ice cream.
Makes 150 ml (¼ pint)

BUTTERSCOTCH SAUCE

142 ml (5 fl oz) double cream
50 g (2 oz) unsalted butter
75 g (3 oz) soft dark brown sugar

Place the cream, butter and sugar in a pan. Heat gently, stirring, until the sugar has dissolved. Boil for 2 minutes until syrupy. Serve warm, with vanilla ice cream or profiteroles.
Makes 250 ml (8 fl oz)

VANILLA CREAM SAUCE

3 egg yolks
1 tablespoon caster sugar
300 ml (½ pint) milk
split vanilla pod or ½ teaspoon vanilla essence

Blend the egg yolks and sugar in a small bowl. Heat the milk and vanilla pod, or essence, until boiling. Discard the vanilla pod, if used, and pour the milk onto the egg yolks, stirring.
    Return the mixture to the pan and heat very gently, stirring, until thick enough to coat the back of a spoon; do not allow to boil. Strain the sauce into a jug and serve hot or cold. This sauce makes a delicious accompaniment to meringue desserts.
Makes about 300 ml (½ pint)

Butterscotch Sauce; Melba Sauce; Fudge Sauce; Apricot Sauce; Chocolate Sauce; Mincemeat Sauce

FUDGE SAUCE

1 × 170 g (6 oz) can evaporated milk
50 g (2 oz) plain chocolate
50 g (2 oz) soft brown sugar

Place the ingredients in a small pan and heat gently, stirring, until the sugar has dissolved. Bring to the boil, then simmer for 2 to 3 minutes. Serve warm or cold, with vanilla, chocolate, coffee or maple and walnut ice cream.
Makes 250 ml (8 fl oz)

YOUR OWN FAVOURITE DESSERTS

Although you will find dessert recipes for every occasion in this colourful collection, you will most certainly come across exciting culinary ideas elsewhere – from radio and television programmes, magazines, store leaflets and friends, of course. All too often we jot these down on odd pieces of paper or tear pages out of magazines – only to discover they are lost when needed!

Use the following pages to record your own favourite desserts, and tried and tested variations on the recipes in this book, together with any time-saving hints.

INDEX

ACKNOWLEDGMENTS

The publishers would like to thank the following individuals who were involved in the preparation of material for this book:
All photography by Paul Williams, except pages 121, 132, 133 and 135 by Roger Phillips

Photographic Stylist: Penny Markham

Food for photography prepared by Carole Handslip and Caroline Ellwood

Designed by Sue Storey